CULTURE/METACULTURE

Culture passes into the twenty-first century as a key word in contemporary critical thought. However, it continues to mean many different things to many different people. *Culture/Metaculture* introduces and analyses the changing definitions of this crucial term.

The author begins by examining the European tradition of Kulturkritik, which, in the wake of the First World War, offered minority culture as the antidote to 'mass' modernity. He then charts key challenges to this conception of culture, beginning in the 1930s and culminating in post-war theories of popular culture. This is followed by a detailed analysis of the rise of Cultural Studies. While Kulturkritik had found its version of culture in the literary canon, the discipline of Cultural Studies grew up around discussions of the media, contemporary politics, ethnicity and Marxism. The work concludes with a brilliant discussion of 'metaculture', or the ways in which culture, however defined, speaks of itself.

Francis Mulhern's interdisciplinary study reveals fascinating links between key political issues and the many definitions of culture. The result is an unrivalled introduction to a concept at the very heart of the new critical idiom.

Francis Mulhern is Professor of Critical Studies at Middlesex University, UK. He is author of *The Moment of Scrutiny* (1979) and *The Present Lasts a Long Time* (1998).

THE NEW CRITICAL IDIOM

SERIES EDITOR: JOHN DRAKAKIS, UNIVERSITY OF STIRLING

The New Critical Idiom is an invaluable series of introductory guides to today's critical terminology. Each book:

- provides a handy, explanatory guide to the use (and abuse) of the term
- offers an original and distinctive overview by a leading literary and cultural critic
- relates the term to the larger field of cultural representation.

With a strong emphasis on clarity, lively debate and the widest possible breadth of examples, *The New Critical Idiom* is an indispensable approach to key topics in literary studies.

Other books in this series:
Colonialism/Postcolonialism by Ania Loomba
Discourse by Sara Mills
Gothic by Fred Botting
Historicism by Paul Hamilton
Humanism by Tony Davies
Ideology by David Hawkes
Intertextuality by Graham Allen
Literature by Peter Widdowson
Metre, Rhythm and Verse Form by Philip Hobsbaum
Myth by Laurence Coupe
Pastoral by Terry Gifford
Romanticism by Aidan Day
Sexuality by Joseph Bristow
Stylistics by Richard Bradford
The Unconscious by Antony Easthope

CULTURE/
METACULTURE

Francis Mulhern

LONDON AND NEW YORK

First published 2000
by Routledge
11 New Fetter Lane, London EC4P 4EE

Simultaneously published in the USA and Canada
by Routledge
29 West 35th Street, New York, NY 10001

Routledge is an imprint of the Taylor & Francis Group

Typeset in Garamond by Taylor & Francis Books Ltd
Printed and bound in Great Britain by Clays Ltd, St Ives PLC

British Library Cataloguing in Publication Data
A catalogue record for this book is available from the British Library

Library of Congress Cataloging in Publication Data
Mulhern, Francis.
 Culture/metaculture / Francis Mulhern.
 p. cm
 Includes bibliographical references and index.
 1. Culture. I. Title.
 HM621 .M85 2000
 306—dc21   99-054750

ISBN 0–415–10229–4 (hbk)
ISBN 0–415–10230–8 (pbk)

CONTENTS

PART II
CULTURAL STUDIES

PART III
METACULTURE AND SOCIETY

SERIES EDITOR'S PREFACE

The New Critical Idiom is a series of introductory books which seeks to extend the lexicon of literary terms, in order to address the radical changes which have taken place in the study of literature during the last decades of the twentieth century. The aim is to provide clear, well-illustrated accounts of the full range of terminology currently in use, and to evolve histories of its changing usage.

The current state of the discipline of literary studies is one where there is considerable debate concerning basic questions of terminology. This involves, among other things, the boundaries which distinguish the literary from the non-literary; the position of literature within the larger sphere of culture; the relationship between literatures of different cultures; and questions concerning the relation of literary to other cultural forms within the context of interdisciplinary studies.

It is clear that the field of literary criticism and theory is a dynamic and heterogeneous one. The present need is for individual volumes on terms which combine clarity of exposition with an adventurousness of perspective and a breadth of application. Each volume will contain as part of its apparatus some indication of the direction in which the definition of particular terms is likely to move, as well as expanding the disciplinary boundaries within which some of these terms have been traditionally contained. This will involve some re-situation of terms within the larger field of cultural representation, and will introduce examples from the area of film and the modern media in addition to examples from a variety of literary texts.

ACKNOWLEDGEMENTS

John Drakakis generously invited me to write this book, and still more generously bore with my tardiness in completing it; for this and for his critical encouragement and advice, my warm thanks to him.

Some parts of the book, and versions of its general argument, were first aired in seminar papers; for these opportunities I have to thank Mick Jardine, Maria Elisa Cevasco and Tadhg Foley, and their respective colleagues at King Alfred's University College, Winchester, the University of São Paulo, and the National University of Ireland, Galway.

Pilot versions of the general argument appeared in *Travesia* (now *Journal of Latin American Cultural Studies*) and *Monthly Review*. I am grateful to the editors of those journals, and particularly to John Kraniauskas and Ellen Meiksins Wood. I have reiterated some of the material of 'A welfare culture?', published in *Radical Philosophy* 77, May–June 1996, for which I thank the editors.

Rachel Malik and Peter Osborne have been models of critical support: to them, my special thanks.

INTRODUCTION

Culture has long been said to be a rare and a vulnerable thing, but no one could speak likewise of the discussion it inspires, which, in contrast, has never been more prolific or robust. Familiar modern understandings of the term persist, more or less strongly: culture as a storehouse of essentially human or essentially national values. But they persist now in more or less radical tension with the newer understanding of culture as the ordinary social, historical world of sense, of 'symbolic' or meaning-bearing activity in all its forms. 'Culture' in that expanded, secular definition has imprinted itself on a whole range of disciplines: history and sociology, for example, and literary studies, where the older meanings have been fundamental, and above all Cultural Studies itself. It follows that no one venturing to add a further volume to the library of contemporary writing in the area should expect the hospitality once readily accorded to travellers from faraway places. Readers will wish to know in what this book differs from others near to hand. My subject is the discussion itself, 'culture' as a topic in twentieth-century debate, in Europe and particularly in Britain.

A topic, in old, strict usage, is not merely what is spoken of – an object real or imagined: it is an established object of discussion with established terms of treatment. Thus, a topic is always already a convention, implying a settled relationship between those who participate in it. The most successful topics achieve the status of commonplaces, a metaphor we do well to take literally. In the words of the French sociologist Pierre Bourdieu, they are 'those places in discourse in which an entire group meets and recognizes itself' (1993: 168). The 'place' I wish to explore here is the one called *culture*: that is 'culture' *as the topic* of some major intellectual traditions of the past century. My own redescription of that topic, which I intend also as a critical displacement of it, is *metaculture*, or *metacultural discourse*. The purpose of the following paragraphs is to introduce these and other key elements in the conceptual vocabulary of the book, and in this way to outline its argument.

Most varieties of discourse identified by the Greek prefix *meta-* (literally, 'after' or 'with') will have one and often two distinctive characteristics. They will be concerned with the most general and fundamental problems in their domain – thus, Freud reserved the term 'metapsychology' for his most systematic theoretical accounts of mental life. And they will be more or less strongly reflexive, being themselves a part of what they speak of – thus, 'metafiction' designates a kind of fiction about fiction. Metacultural discourse, then, is that in which culture, however defined, speaks of itself. More precisely, it is discourse in which culture addresses its own generality and conditions of existence. All four terms in this formulation need emphasis. It is the *generality* of sense-making activity that is in question, not merely one or another of its many specific varieties, say, religious worship or window-shopping or poetry or adult education. That generality is addressed in its social–historical *conditions of existence*, which may be conceptualized, for example, as 'industrialism', or 'capitalism', or 'modernity'. Metaculture is *discourse* in the strong sense of that versatile term: a historically formed set of topics and procedures that both drives and regulates the utterance of the individuals who inhabit it, and assigns them definite positions in the field of meaning it delimits. The position of seeing and speaking and writing in metacultural discourse, the kind of subject any individual 'becomes' in practising it, is *culture itself*. There will be more to say shortly. For now, let me stress that no one, to my knowledge, has ever described themselves as a practitioner of 'metacultural discourse'. The term and the concept have emerged from the critical work of writing this book. If any one term or reference or affiliation might be said to link all the writers discussed here – and in bare truth there is none – it would be the more familiar *culture*.

One term, but hardly one meaning – the very phrase 'culture itself' seems unwarrantable. 'Culture' has designated quite distinct and sometimes mutually foreign fields of practice and inquiry, and has graced the banners of radically opposed causes. The largely chronological sequencing of this book, from 1918 to the near-present, does not imply a simple narrative of progress (or decline). Its main principle of organization is comparative, foregrounding two mutually antagonistic traditions of discourse on culture – Kulturkritik and Cultural Studies – terms that must themselves be clarified here. The first is much older. The second took shape in conscious opposition to it. But my chief critical interest lies in the evidence of continuity between them, in the conceptual *form* they appear to have in common. Here is the sense in which the singular 'culture itself' is perhaps not so ambiguous after all.

The German term *Kulturkritik* passes literally into English as 'cultural criticism'. However, this simple translation creates conceptual confusion. The English phrase is in widespread use as a general term denoting any kind of formal discussion of any activity thought of as cultural: literary criticism, film reviews, fashion commentaries of a certain kind, homilies on contemporary sexual mores are so many instances of cultural criticism in this familiar, spacious sense. However, the historical meaning of *Kulturkritik* is much narrower. For that reason – for the sake of simplicity, in fact – I have preferred to import it directly (and to print it, henceforward, without its foreignizing italics) as a term that is both adequately general and properly restrictive, and thus critically exact. Kulturkritik, in its classic European form, took shape in the later eighteenth century as a critical, normally negative discourse on the emerging symbolic universe of capitalism, democracy and enlightenment – on the values of a condition and process of social life for which a recent French coinage furnished the essential term: *civilisation* (Febvre 1973: 219–57). Germany was the continental heartland of this discourse: it was in the philosophical histories of Johann Gottfried von Herder that *Zivilisation* was first questioned in the name of *Kultur* ([1774] 1969: 179–224). The second major European centre of Kulturkritik was England, whose counterpart tradition is the subject of Raymond Williams's classic study, *Culture and Society*. 'The basic element' in this discourse, Williams concluded there, 'is its effort at total qualitative assessment ... of the whole form of our common life' ([1958] 1961: 285) – or what I have termed the 'generality' of symbolic life and its historical 'conditions of existence'. The critical resources for that effort were confirmed by the poet Matthew Arnold, in the 1680s, as 'culture'. Culture, for Arnold, was a normative value: it was 'the best which has been thought and said in the world', 'the passion for sweetness and light', 'the study of perfection', harmonious and general; it was 'right reason' concerned to 'know the object as in itself it really is' ([1869] 1932). Although developmental in character, culture was universal in its moral scope and application, emerging from and directed towards what was distinctively human in humanity, the 'best self' that might qualify and even overrule the 'ordinary selves' of everyday class and other social interests. It was the spiritual basis of a possible civil order, as binding in its sphere, and, ideally, as commanding as the state itself.[1] Culture, in this construction, is not merely a repository of value: it is the *principle* of a good society. Arnold's statement of the cultural principle, as it can pointedly be called, became classic in English-language Kulturkritik in the twentieth century.[2] Yet his assumption that the norms of culture were necessarily those of universal humanity is not typical of the tradition more widely seen. Herder, too, valued *Humanität* and its development, but the 'culture' that mediated that 'human-ness' was, for him, always in reality plural and historically relative. Cultures were the symbolic forms of life of human groups, shaped in diverse conditions and growing into new shapes as they encountered new demands and opportunities. The civilizing process could not, or should not, uproot these equally though differently 'human' cultures, whose most important emerging variety was the nation. 'Human nature is not the vessel of an absolute, unchanging and independent happiness, as defined by the philosopher. ... Even the image of happiness changes with each condition and climate. ... each nation has its centre of gravity within itself, just as every sphere has its centre of gravity' (Herder [1774] 1969: 185–6). Here, too, is the cultural principle. Of course, this romantic counter-emphasis on culture-as-national-value, as the 'traditional' virtue of a people, seems incompatible with Arnold's humanism. But intellectual history does not follow the rules of logic textbooks, and, as we shall see, twentieth-century Kulturkritik sustained both varieties of 'culture' and produced hybrids of the two, all of them sharing a single discursive form.

The greater historical impact of Herder's thought was registered elsewhere, however, in the emergence of an array of discourses on 'culture' as what T.S. Eliot would call 'a whole way of life'. The world-transforming power of nationalism, from the mid-nineteenth century into our continuing present, has ensured the universal currency of 'culture' in this sense – as, in effect, ethnic custom. In the field of formalized intellectual inquiry, its main sponsor, until the later twentieth century, was anthropology. 'Cultural' or 'social' anthropology, the settled names for a pursuit first proposed as simple 'culturology', took shape as the putative science of the 'superorganic': of learned rather than instinctive behaviour, or, more strictly, the 'symboling' life of societies (White 1975). 'Culture' in this sense might indeed be valued (according to the lights and purposes of the visiting anthropologist) but it was not, in Arnold's general sense, a normative value, a precious human endowment of spiritual capital. It was the totality of symbolic life in a given social space. Anthropology itself lies beyond the range of this study. However, Eliot's phrase is only one among many illustrations of its exemplary status in the wider intellectual life of the past century, and, specifically, of the inspirational value it was assigned in the formation of a new discourse on culture in mid-century Britain – what came to be called cultural studies. That lineage of cultural studies (which, in this book, I spell with initial capitals, except where my intended reference is not only to the academic practice so named) emerged in a complex process that was both a continuation and a displacement of English Kulturkritik. The theoretical stakes in that process have a major part in what follows here, and for now I will indicate only as much as may serve to move these introductory remarks towards their conclusion. Cultural studies has evolved more than once (Carey 1997; Frow and Morris 1993). It has more or less established positions throughout the English-speaking world, and has now extended its reach well beyond them. Its niche, it seems, is the planet. The critical account I develop here is based on the British case, which, I know, is not the beginning and end of all possible cultural studies. At the same time, that variety has thus far enjoyed greater international currency than any other, and even if it has no special claim to global authority, its record deserves particular attention. For the same reason, the arguments advanced here have implications reaching beyond the British setting.

Cultural Studies has favoured a radical expansion of the field of relevant inquiry, and a strictly egalitarian ethic of attention within it. Any form or practice of signification is in principle eligible, without any presumptive test of 'quality'. But these are studies with a mission that is not merely sociological or anthropological. The justifying purpose of Cultural Studies has been to revoke the historic privileges of 'culture with a capital C' (the sovereign value of Kulturkritik) and vindicate the active meanings and values of the subordinate majority (the so-called 'masses') as core elements of a possible alternative order. 'Power' is indissociable from meaning, in this perspective, which is thus necessarily 'political' (Hall 1997). My argument will be that Cultural Studies is prone to misrecognize itself: that its predominant tendency has been to negate the specific social values of Kulturkritik while retaining their deep form, which it therefore repeats as the pattern of its own strategic imagination. The co-ordinates of that form are *culture, authority* and *politics*.

In both versions, *culture* is the object but also, and crucially, the subject, the ideal subject, of discourse. It is the cultural principle itself (be it elite or popular) that furnishes the conditions of seeing and speaking, that determines what I see and speak of, and as what 'I' do so. In keeping with this, the cultural principle also sets the conditions of ethically valid intellectual practice: meta-cultural discourse is normally, among other things, a reflection on the meaning of intellectual vocation. The ultimate stake, in all cases, is social *authority*. 'Power', in the indiscriminate sense that has been standard in Cultural Studies, is a blunt instrument of scant theoretical value here. Injunctive social practices – those of command and control in the broadest senses – take a variety of forms, including the sanctions deriving from the ownership and control of property and, at the extreme, physical coercion, for which the term 'power' is perhaps best reserved. Cultural injunction is typically not of that kind: its dominant mode is *authority*, which is itself predominantly cultural in substance. Authority relations are those in which assent is secured on non-coercive grounds. The mark of authority, as a form of injunction, is that it normally appears as if granted by those who defer to it. Metacultural discourse lodges a polemical authority claim of the most general kind, in respect of social relations as a whole: the cultural principle is the basis of public virtue. The socially con-trasted ideal subjects of Kulturkritik and Cultural Studies are alike in this: both urge 'culture' as the necessary, unregarded truth of society, whose curse is the inadequacy of the prevailing form of general authority, *the political*. It is politics as such that is fundamentally in question here: in declared principle, in the case of Kulturkritik, or as a self-defeating final implication, in the case of Cultural Studies. The latter's 'political' assault on high-cultural privilege has turned out to be, at the same time, a renewed attempt at a 'cultural' dissolution of politics – a popular-leftist mutation of metacultural discourse.

The evidence for these bald claims, and the elaborated, more nuanced arguments they depend upon, are the substance of this book. Part I begins with a discussion of European Kulturkritik, in its diverse national sensibilities and intellectual formats. The novelist Thomas Mann, the philosophers Julien Benda and José Ortega y Gasset, the sociologist Karl Mannheim and the literary critic F.R. Leavis are brought together as classic critics of 'mass' modernity between the First and Second World Wars. Sigmund Freud, Virginia Woolf, George Orwell and assorted Marxisms then illustrate the stresses to which the common assumptions of such criticism were subject in the 1930s. T.S. Eliot and Richard Hoggart define the new terms of cultural reflection in post-war Britain. The crucial work of Raymond Williams enables a critical retrospect on the tradition of Kulturkritik and the break into a new way of theorizing culture. Cultural studies, broadly understood, is the second major tradition discussed here. Part II reconstructs the conceptual formation of Cultural Studies, focusing particularly on the British tradition. Stuart Hall and his collaborators at the Birmingham Centre for Cultural Studies come to the fore here, in discussions of media analysis, contemporary politics, ethnicity, Marxism and the controversy over 'populism' in the analysis of culture. Throughout this discussion of Cultural Studies, my critical priority is to elicit its discoverable relations with Kulturkritik, the tradition it has struggled against, and to elucidate its opaque ambivalence towards the tradition of theory and politics to which it owes its existence, namely Marxism. The unifying theme of Parts I and II is the relationship between culture, in its conflicting senses, and the idea of politics. The concluding part of the book is devoted to a general analysis, both formal and historical, of the logic of metaculture – the utopian impulse, common to the old cultural criticism and the new cultural studies, to resolve the tension of the relationship between culture and politics by dissolving political reason itself.

Seen as a whole, then, the book is historical in procedure: metacultural discourse is understood as an entity shaped and reshaped in determinate social conditions. Its governing question is critical. What has been the form and logic of that discourse and how far is it valid? The form of that question, which is general, in turn dictates the thematic proportions of the book: the older and newer preoccupations of Kulturkritik and Cultural Studies – the large issues of markets, classes, gender, sexuality, race and postcoloniality, to name the most salient ones – are present here, but not as independent headings of discussion. There are many books that offer a tour of the syllabus in their field, but this is not one of them. I emphasize this point, believing that there are few easier paths into difficulty than the one paved with fixed expectations.

Two further remarks may prove helpful. Critical commentaries are as much works in themselves as the texts they discuss – they may be worthless but that is another question – and cannot seriously be offered, or safely be taken as labour-saving substitutes for them. And when, as in this case, the individual commentaries function as stages in a single, continuous argument, the order of reading becomes crucial. The book has been written as a considered whole, and asks to be read as such, in its given sequence – which, indeed, is the most accessible way through it. In keeping with the developing scheme for the series in which the book appears, I have appended a short glossary – not as a would-be substitute for dictionaries and wider reading but as a convenient checklist for readers who may be unfamiliar with some of the core terminology and conceptual references of the text.

PART I

KULTURKRITIK

1

AGAINST MASS CIVILIZATION

Between the outbreak of the First World War in 1914 and the conclusion of the Second World War in 1945, Europe underwent one of the most convulsive general transformations in its history. The killing factories of the Great War did not run on blood and money alone: they devoured constitutions, social orders, traditions – whole ways of life. After thirty years of armed conflict in and among the societies of the continent, fought amid economic disorder and feverish cultural agitation, little remained of Europe's long nineteenth century. In the middle years of this long, complex sequence, it seemed evident that something was nearing its end. The struggles to interpret and perhaps affect that outcome form the cultural history of the time.

An adequate account would emphasize the incongruous experience of inter-war capitalism, which saw brilliant developments in the repertoire of production – the new world of automobiles, radio and cinema – but also chaos in finance and trade; the impotence of liberal parliaments in the face of domestic and international disorder; the challenge of organized labour and, above all, its revolutionary communist left; and the march of fascism (Hobsbawm 1994). In most interpretations, then and later, these political manifestations illustrated the ultimate terms of choice. But in another perspective, they were no more than variant instances of a single, fundamentally coherent and probably irresistible historical tendency. For one kind of intellectual, the practitioner of Kulturkritik, the historic stake was the future of *culture* in the epoch of modernity, whose culminating feature, now manifest, was the rise of *the masses*, the distinctive life-form of *civilization*. Five classic statements define this high-minded rally against the new times. Five distinguished writers – one German, one French, one Hungarian, one Spanish, one English – embody its prophetic style: Thomas Mann, Julien Benda, Karl Mannhein, José Ortega y Gasset and F.R. Leavis. Together, they substantiate the underlying unity of Kulturkritik.

THE UNPOLITICAL THOMAS MANN

Thomas Mann's *Betrachtungen eines Unpolitischen*, or 'reflections of an unpolitical man', was written during the First World War, and appeared in its last weeks.[1] Mann is of course best known for his novels, and for his leading part in the intellectual resistance to fascism. In the *Reflections*, however, he expressed himself as a German patriot concerned to explain, as if in an 'uninhibited ... private letter', why his country must not submit to France and Britain ([1918] 1983a: 7). Mann's wartime nationalism is not, here and now, the chief interest of his essay (though his casual racism is memorable, and, as we will see, the theme of national–racial identity cannot be marginalized as an unfortunate period extravagance). What is important is that he saw in Germany's war against the western allies the last stand of a traditionalist order against the subversive spiritual forces of modernity,[2] or in the terms that were already classic in German idiom, of 'culture' against 'civilization'.

The opposition between German Kultur and French civilization marked every aspect of the two societies. For all its avowedly personal, essayistic character, Mann's discourse was regular to the point of schematism:

Germany	*France (and Britain)*
culture/Kultur	civilization
art (= poetry, music)	literature (= prose)
protestantism	universalism
burgher	bourgeois
national feeling	humanitarianism
pessimism	progressivism
life	society
irony	radicalism
reverence	enlightenment
inwardness	reason
people	'class and mass'
aristocracy	democracy
ethics	politics

Mann's text set these binaries in an abstract, quasi-musical play of elaboration and variation, with the aim of showing the moral cohesion of each of the two national sets, and the irreducible opposition between them. Thus, he maintained, Kultur was intrinsically national, whereas civilization on the French model was not a development of a national culture but the liquidation of it. Civilization is 'what all nations have in common'. Indeed it could not even claim so much, for the nation, not some programmatic 'humanity', was the true 'bearer of the general, of the human quality' (Mann 1983a: 179). It would be misconceived to challenge French radicalism, with its commitment to systematic programmes of social change, in the name of a political alternative – 'as if the political attitude were not always one and the same: the democratic one' (p. 15). Politics as such was the end of personal inwardness, being 'participation in the state, zeal and passion for the state'. Democracy was 'the state for novels', or 'literature', which, as 'linguistically articulated intellect', was the antithesis of Kultur (p. 218). Democracy was *'finis musicae*, ... the end of music' (pp. 23, 200).

France, then, did not merely represent a contrasting, and now hostile, national culture: rather it most fully represented the historical tendencies that would extinguish national feeling and Kultur as modes of existence. Across the battle lines were ranged the forms of an alien future. Defeat would mean 'conversion' to civilization, the spiritual triumph not merely of the military victors but of their internal collaborators, Germany's 'literary men', with their corrosive, 'nihilistic' enthusiasm for progress and democracy. (Mann's prototypical 'literary man' was his own brother, Heinrich, at the time the more influential novelist of the two.) However, it might be that German irony could moderate the radical probabilities of the future. Irony, in Mann's definition, was 'the self-betrayal of the intellect in favour of life' – in other words, the opposite of the 'radical' belief in consistency at all costs. 'Is truth an argument', he asked, 'when life is at stake?' (pp. 13, 49) And in that spirit, turning to reflect on the prospect of universal suffrage, he suggested that such a reform need not entail capitulation to 'democracy', that life might yet outwit radical intellect. An ideal suffrage, answering to tradition, would be 'aristocratic, ingeniously graduated'. If general voting rights must be conceded, it was only because 'in a sphere in which it is impossible to give each his own, nothing else remains but to give everyone the same' (p. 194). Yet, the democratic effects of the reform, an egalitarian pretence fostering 'the tumult of party campaigns', might be tempered by another innovation that seemed progressive but need not be: 'the freest opportunity for education' would promote the formation of an aristocracy of merit such as Nietzsche had urged. And the governing value of this education would be 'reverence' for the national character with its 'inward' sensibility, not 'French' enlightenment but German traditionalism (p. 187). Forming a type quite opposed to 'civilization's literary man' driven by the itch to reason and reform, the authentically German intellectual would embody the 'suprapolitical, powerfully ethical moment' of Kultur, would be that paradoxical representative figure, the 'unpolitical man'.[3]

JULIEN BENDA, CLERC

The critic and philosopher Julien Benda appeared to confirm Mann's comparative geography of mind. He militantly opposed all forms of romanticism in art and philosophy, deploring the loss of the eighteenth century's classical ethos. He abominated any appeal to patriotic affinity in intellectual affairs – this was 'essentially a German invention' (Benda [1928] 1969). Indeed he went further, rejecting humanitarian and internationalist programmes as mock-universal particularisms of the same kind. His formative public experience had been the controversy over the trial and imprisonment of a Jewish army officer on false charges of espionage, the Dreyfus Affair of the 1890s, which pitted universal against nationalist values in a mythic civil war of France's intelligentsia. Kultur was the epitome of everything he fought against. 'Irony' is not a word that will occur to any reader in connection with his writing, which on the contrary was 'radical' and 'dogmatic' in its assertion of objective, perennial values. He was, in a single, sufficient word, 'French'.

For Benda, the crisis of modernity was that of the ethics of intellectual life. Betrayal – treachery or treason – was the charge that he laid against the intellectuals of the new century in his famous polemic of 1928, *La Trahison des clercs*. He might more pointedly have chosen 'heresy' as the term of indictment, for in setting aside the modern noun *intellectuel* in favour of the anachronistic *clerc*, or man in holy orders, he committed a whole social category to an imprescriptible code of belief and conduct, whose model was medieval priesthood.[4] Benda's *clercs* formed 'a corporation whose only religion is that of justice and of truth' (Benda [1928] 1969: 57, translation amended). For most of 2,000 years, intellect and learning had served 'the ideal', renouncing all individual or group self-assertion (p. 37) – the contrasting 'realism' of ordinary existence. Where intellectuals entered public controversy, it was as Emile Zola had intervened in the Dreyfus affair crying *J'Accuse!*, to defend 'eternal', 'disinterested or metaphysical' values against worldly degradation. Increasingly over the past century, however, their conduct had deteriorated. No longer aloof from social 'passions', they not only responded to their temptations but sought even to inflame them. The language of eternity now 'divinized' the basest desires of everyday life.

'Passion', Benda's word, had also been Mann's, and for all their differences of intellectual genealogy and affinity, the object of his criticism was the same. Mann would not have seconded Benda's indiscriminate equation of race, nation and class as objects of love or loathing, but he had already traced the threat to Kultur to the phenomenon that Benda now identified as the enemy of intellectual virtue. Modernity was 'essentially the age of politics', and the specific treachery of the modern *clerc* was to have adapted to it, not restraining but 'perfecting' that 'passion', in 'the age of the *intellectual organization of political hatreds*' (Benda [1928] 1969: 27). The favouring conditions of this modern development were economic and constitutional. The relative easing of material conditions encouraged fuller exploration of social possibilities, with material gain itself now established as a key index of human value. With the weakening of aristocratic prerogatives came a new style of political rule, in which popular sentiment exerted an unprecedented force. These tendencies came together in the commercial press, and conspired to fashion a new intellectual ethos whose epitome was 'the cheap daily political newspaper'. The *clercs*, sustained at one time by 'enlightened patronage', now depended on the market in print; they wrote not for 'peers' but for 'the masses', 'the crowds': thus it was that 'no one writes with impunity in a democracy' (pp. 9–10, 112). The cumulative effect of these developments, Benda charged, was the overthrow of the humanly proper order of social authority. Plato, in Antiquity, had assumed the primacy of morality over politics. For Machiavelli, on the cusp of early modernity, these were separate realms. The *clercs* of the twentieth century made philosophy out of circumstance, rewriting virtue as expediency, morality as a gloss on political interest. Benda's personal political choices, when he felt obliged to make them, were liberal; and he was later to conclude that democracy was the only political principle that was compatible with the values of the true *clerc* (Benda 1975: 81). But the logic of his general position was ascetic and reclusive: in a world governed by the 'realistic' urges of majorities, authority resided anywhere except in the timeless truth of the mind, the ideal zone that was his equivalent of the homeland of Kulturkritik.

KARL MANNHEIM'S INTELLECTUALS

Karl Mannheim shared Benda's conviction that the crux of modern culture lay in the disordering of a consensual role for intellectuals, specifically in their relationship with politics. The themes of intellectual fanaticism and cynicism that drove Benda's polemic returned in the sociological argument of his *Ideology and Utopia* (Mannheim 1936). Again like Benda, and also like his adoptive compatriot Thomas Mann, Mannheim saw the crisis as historical, as the upshot of the disintegration of a traditional society characterized by hierarchy and limited mobility, and sustaining forms of political and cultural authority that owed nothing to the goodwill of voters or markets. However, in a perspective like Mannheim's, both men were vulnerable to charges of dogmatism: Benda for his adherence to 'static' ideals, which were, as his own medievalizing idiom attested, abstracted relics of the feudal order, with its 'closed and thoroughly organized stratum of intellectuals' (1936: 10), Mann for his traditionalist commitment to an essentially 'German' collective sensibility. Historically relativistic in a way that was anathema to Benda, and rationalistic in a style quite foreign to Mann, Mannheim affirmed the possibility of a progressive political–cultural outcome. His specific purpose was to elucidate the conditions and objects of a public role for intellectuals that would be coherent, principled and practical, with benign social potential. Writing from Weimar Germany, where he had gone after the defeat of the Hungarian Revolution of 1919, and from a disciplinary base in the sociology of knowledge, of which he was a leading practitioner, Mannheim proposed a distinctive strategic function for intellectuals as such, in a 'scientific politics'.

Intensifying class consciousness was the hallmark of the present, Mannheim believed, and political culture was more and more fully organized according to the priorities of mutually antagonistic 'party schools'. Against these partisan schemes of social value, he set the possibility of a 'forum' that would 'safeguard ... the perspective of and the interest in the whole' (p. 144). In Mannheim's reasoning, this appeal to an overarching general interest – 'the whole' as a possible and desirable intellectual allegiance – did not presuppose a 'static' realm of objective truths beyond history (as it did for Benda) and did not imply only a preference for social compromise. The principle of his sociology was that all knowledge, and especially political knowledge, was 'interest-bound', and that the major social classes – workers and bourgeoisie alike – 'have their outlooks and activities directly and exclusively determined by their specific social situations' (p. 140). But in the case of the intelligentsia, the effects of this determinism were paradoxical. As a stratum, intellectuals were mixed in class provenance and situation. Their only social common denominator was *education*, the site on which all the rival interests and ideologies of society confronted one another. The education system (specifically, universities and specialized institutions of higher learning) was an everyday constituent assembly of the mind, so to say, in which competing social knowledges might enter a process of 'dynamic mediation' and 'synthesis', for the common good. And in this lay the appropriate political function of the intelligentsia, the possibility of fulfilling 'their mission as the predestined advocate of the intellectual interests of the whole', and thus resolving the cultural crisis of modernity (p. 140).

This prophetic idiom of 'mission' and 'destiny', which sounds odd in a would-be scientific discourse, suggests an activist version of Benda: a clerisy indeed, but in this case positively committed to public affairs. However, the flow of Mannheim's reasoning was disturbed by a cross-current of pessimism. Claiming to deduce the politics of the intelligentsia from the objective tendencies of the modern social order, and, above all, the logic of its education system, he nevertheless conceded that its implementation 'in an epoch like our own' was 'scarcely ... possible'. The missionaries would probably be destined for altogether more desperate duties, as 'watchmen in what otherwise would be a pitch-black night' (p. 143). This is the understandable rhetoric of a liberal in the later days of the Weimar Republic, but its logic is that of a wider discursive context. Mannheim's sociology was relativist, seeing 'ideas' as translations of 'interests' – fundamentally, class interests – whose power of cultural determination was, for most cases, unqualified. At the same time, he canvassed a politics whose defining value was an attainable reconciliation of interests, a 'predestined' discovery, not merely of a structured totality of relationships but of a deep wholeness. The educational practice of intellectuals furnished the warrant and the means of this mission. Yet Mannheim emphasized that intellectuals were neither a class nor a supra-class stratum. They formed a mixed-class entity united only by educational values. And in nominating them as a potentially decisive political agency, he was entrusting the work of 'synthesis' to a possibility that his general theory appeared to discount in principle: an idea whose motivating social interest was itself an idea. In this basic respect, Mannheim's sociological reasoning ran parallel with Benda's philosophical dualism of 'ideal' and 'real' values, and was bound by direct discursive affiliation to

Mann's Kulturkritik – on the one hand a driven world of material interests and their validating ideologies, civilization sightless in the dark or blinded by artificial lights; on the other, Kultur, the essential, now homeless values of the human spirit.

Mannheim's greater confidence in a habitable future only testified the more strongly to his kinship with Benda and Mann. In his vision of a specifically intellectual politics of the whole, he reanimated, for the twentieth century, the figure of a medieval clerisy, which was the ground of Benda's thought.[5] The proposed ascent from the party schools to the forum of mediation was not so much a form of engagement in ordinary political space as an attempt to supervene over it, from a higher plane of social judgement. The activist intellectual mediator was a version, now improbably powerful, of the unpolitical man.

ORTEGA'S ARISTOCRATIC VISION

José Ortega y Gasset offered a characteristically more truculent summary of the contemporary peril. In the phrase that his book of 1930 made famous, it was 'the revolt of the masses'. Ortega was prepared to concede that the historical prospect remained undecided: 'in itself it contains the twin potencies of triumph or death' (1932: 59). Recent decades had seen an unprecedented 'rise in the historic level' of human potentiality. Liberal democracy and 'technicism' (that is, industry plus experimental science) had dramatically extended the scope of material, mental and moral life, tripling Europe's population in less than a century, promoting the idea of 'rights' as the key term of social intercourse and political participation, and, above all, filling the world with 'things' of every kind. These trends represented an undeniable 'quantitative advance', and might indeed support 'the transition to some new, unexampled organization of humanity' (pp. 15, 29–33, 39). But the sea rises also, and furnishes the metaphor of rising level as deluge; the ascent of the masses '*may* also be a catastrophe of human destiny' (pp. 18, 59). Ortega was resigned to the darker probability. The great phenomenon of the time, for him, was 'the accession of the masses to complete social power', and there was no doubt where their spontaneous inclinations would lead them (p. 9).

Ortega's sardonic, worldly manner, contrasting with Mann's inwardness, Mannheim's scientific mien and Benda's rhetoric of detachment, was that of a writer who was not only a philosopher but a journalist and, for a time, a parliamentarian; and the urgency of his polemic owed something to the deepening crisis in his own country, Spain. But he insisted that his purpose was more than merely political, indeed that it was 'neutral', breathing 'an air much ampler than that of politics and its dissensions' (p. 73). The coming of the masses was not merely a quantitative phenomenon, though as that it was certainly impressive. It did not consist only in the increasing significance of popular mobilization in contemporary politics – though anarchist trade-unions and fascism were objects of particular loathing here. The real novelty and danger lay in the sheer presence of 'the multitude' in social spaces 'hitherto reserved', and the consequent transformation of collective mentality. 'There are no longer protagonists; there is only the chorus' (p. 10). By 'masses', Ortega insisted, he did not merely mean the labouring classes. The 'dynamic unity' of mass and minority defined all social classes. Traditionally, minorities had exercised disproportionate influence in the higher classes, but there too, now, the masses were growing stronger. 'Mass-man' was simply 'the average man', one in whom singularity was absent or decaying, and who in any case depreciated that quality. The masses were 'indifferent' twice over: interchangeable, and unconcerned that they should be so. Inertia, passivity, indiscipline, narcissism and ingratitude were now proliferating in 'an overwhelming and violent moral upheaval', a 'tragic' process inspiring 'terror' and threatening a reversion to 'barbarism' (pp. 17, 40).

Ortega sponsored a 'radically aristocratic interpretation of history'. Society was essentially aristocratic, that is to say, the continuing achievement of minority effort, and in ceasing to be that, ceased to be anything at all (p. 16). It was in this sense that he defended the 'old democracy' against the new. The former had been 'liberal' in respecting the rights and, more important, the prerogatives of minorities. Universal suffrage had functioned once as a means whereby the majority chose between 'minority programmes' for 'collective life' (p. 36). Now it served as the rationale for 'hyperdemocracy', the ignorant, lawless appetite of mass-man in the public domain. Liberal rule had depended on 'public opinion', but this had implied an educated sense of priorities that was foreign to the habits of mass self-assertion (p. 97). The proliferation of human material had overwhelmed the 'traditional' controls (p. 39). Intellectuals could no longer expect to instruct, but must submit to the presumptuous judgement of 'the commonplace mind' (p. 14). Indeed the intellectual function itself had been compromised by the accelerated development of scientific knowledge. The modern figure of the technician – 'actual scientific man' – furnished the prototype of mass-man. Specialization favoured the rise of the 'learned ignoramus' at the expense of the 'cultured' intellectual who, having access to the idea of the whole, could hope to formulate a unifying social vision. Thwarted at every turn by the automatic impulses of mass-man, 'the normal exercise of authority' in culture and politics had become impossible (pp. 86, 97).

The possibility of a renewed authority flickered in Ortega's prose, but was instantly quenched: 'the masses are incapable of submitting to direction of any kind' – could not submit, even if 'for a moment' they mustered 'good will' enough to make the effort. Indeed, it appeared unclear to what spiritual authority they might be urged to submit. For Ortega's parting words disarmingly reframed the argumentation leading up to them. His intuitions of truth were probably not Benda's, but who could confidently say? Deeper than politics, even deeper, it seemed, than 'culture' itself, after more than one hundred pages of acrid cultural diagnosis, the 'great question' concerning modern Europe had not yet been posed.

F.R. LEAVIS'S CRITICAL MINORITY

The blind material impetus of modernity, the increasing scale and indifference of social life, the weakening of traditional values in the face of commonplace enlightenment, the lapse of intellectual standards at the beckoning of worldly advantage, the prospect of a historic loss of the past: this cluster of themes, familiar now from Germany, France and Spain, recurred in the work of England's most compelling cultural critic of the middle century, F.R. Leavis. For Leavis, the modern crisis was that of 'minority culture' in the corrosive environment of 'mass civilization' (these were the titular terms of his pamphlet of 1930, the year of Ortega's *Revolt of the Masses*).[6] The stake was the survival of moral memory – or, for it was the same thing, the health of the English language.

Leavis was an anti-systematic thinker, with a fixed distrust of programmatic statement; there is no convenient epitome to excerpt from his collected works. Yet his critical practice was as systematic as any, and perhaps more programmatic than most. Its conceptual frame was a specific interpretation of the process of modernity, rendered as a narrative of English social history since the seventeenth century. In the two centuries-odd after 1600, a society deserving the name of 'community' had been weakened, disorganized and then irreparably torn apart by the logic of economic change. The defining mentality of community was one in which individual and collective interests were organized by common codes of understanding and valuation; in which the hierarchy of social classes was a binding, not a divisive condition of life, favouring a beneficial cross-fertilization of refined and popular practices; in which custom might alter without convulsion; and in which, therefore, there was a spontaneous tendency towards balance and unity in psychic life and a corresponding 'impersonality' in spoken and written idiom. The sustaining condition of this human order was its agricultural economy, whose typical rate of technical change was never such as to disrupt the practical and symbolic continuities of kinship, place and work, and the codes of value associated with them. The mid-century revolution disrupted this old order and released the social forces that would eventually dissipate its moral reserves. Commercial activity intensified, in a process that led to industrialization, and the extinction of 'community' as a general condition of existence. The social order of meaning and value was henceforward structured by the discrepant, increasingly antagonistic relationship between *culture* – the realm of qualities, moral values, ends – and *civilization* – the domain of quantities and means. This was an unequal relationship, whose necessary course ran contrary to the interests of culture. For civilization was forwarded by an automatic technical dynamic; it was the spontaneous moral sensibility of the industrial economy. Culture, on the other hand, must now subsist in conditions where it could not take root and flourish; it was, by virtue of its commitment to a 'human norm', an exposed survivor, the memory of a common life that had gone forever.

Industrialization, with its new forms of work, consumption and recreation, severed one after another line of cultural continuity, in a process that Leavis summarized as 'standardization' and 'levelling-down' (1933a: 18). Religious sanctions had weakened. Increased mobility and expanding communications had disrupted traditional affiliations. Newspaper and book publishing, joined now by cinema and radio, observed the inflexible demands of the market, and wooed mass urban-industrial audiences with various mixtures of quack enlightenment, stock opinion and formulaic gratification. There remained only one living survivor from a better past – the language in its most developed form, 'the living subtlety of the finest idiom' (p. 40) – and it too was now imperilled.

Leavis's Marxist contemporaries would object that analysis of this kind mistook the cause of the symptoms it deplored, attributing to a technical system, industrial production, what should properly be seen as the working of a specific form of society based on a distinctive form of private property, namely capitalism. Leavis replied that, in the perspective of culture, the difference between capitalism and socialism was 'inessential' (1933a: 1–12, 160–6). Concepts of property had no place in Leavis's understanding of social relations. Common ownership of the means of production, which for Marxists would fundamentally distinguish socialism as a human order, was, for him, a dubious or empty gain, in an epoch whose driving-force was 'the machine'. And in so far as socialism promoted still further industrial development, it would merely accentuate the destructive tendencies of the society it replaced. 'The Marxian future', he wrote, seems 'vacuous, Wellsian and bourgeois' (1933b: 322). Leavis's rejection of socialism, and of Communism as its militant vanguard, was part of a fundamental alienation from politics as such. The dominant tendencies of mass, mechanical civilization were fixed and mutually supporting. Their logic precluded the emergence of a counter-force sufficient to halt or redirect them. An adequate 'political' intervention must be specifically cultural in interest and mode, a mobilization of critical intelligence – of Kulturkritik – for the vindication of 'tradition', the precious touchstones by which contemporary standards of judgement might be authenticated and, where possible, deployed to 'check and control' the stupefying development of 'the machine' and its life-forms.

Leavisian cultural politics was minoritarian, for it was self-contradictory to assume that mass civilization could ever incur majority disapproval. Its favoured instrument was journalism, a mobile, interventionist style of activity consistent with Leavis's sense of principled, 'outlaw' opportunism. Its strategic theatre was education, that space where training for the modern 'machine' had not yet wholly supplanted older traditions of humane learning. Its defining practice was literary criticism. The sectarian brilliance of Leavis's practice as a teacher and critic, and, for two decades after the publication of *Mass Civilization and Minority Culture*, as editor of the quarterly journal *Scrutiny*, became a legend (Mulhern 1979; MacKillop 1995). By the 1960s, he was spoken for and against with vehement conviction in education and literary circles, not only in Britain but throughout the English-speaking world and beyond. The stories go on being told. What must be stressed here, then, against all other considerations, is that Leavis's practice, which has often been trivialized as the expression of a personality, followed with the force of logical deduction from his reading of the modern historical process. Literature, as language in its finest use, was what chiefly remained of a common 'art of living'. But where social spontaneity had once fostered that use of language, it now threatened to stunt it. The mechanized, standardized idioms of mass civilization, the cynical enthusiasms of the publicity apparatus and the genteel or populist tipsters of the book clubs and reviews pages would co-operate to erase literary culture as memory and possibility, and in doing so condemn a mock-literate humanity to a deathly moral amnesia. The future of literature as a living, fertilizing social presence depended on a reassertion of critical standards: on an unsparing effort of discrimination that would revalue the heterogeneous accumulation of the literary past, so as more surely to distinguish the authentic from the fraudulent or merely conventional in the present. This was the special responsibility of literary criticism and the ground of its special authority. For in knowing literature truly, the 'critical minority' knew mass civilization as it could never know itself. Criticism might seem the least powerful of political offices, but none could match its spiritual authority.

THE DISCOURSE OF KULTURKRITIK

A German novelist, a Hungarian emigré sociologist, two philosophers, one French, the other Spanish, and an English literary critic: the differences are manifest, and irreducible. Yet these contrasts recall attention to the more interesting evidence of a common identity. Indeed the grounds of affinity are in four of the five cases genealogical: Mann and Mannheim both descend in the direct line of German romanticism; Leavis in the collateral English line traceable back through Arnold to Coleridge; Ortega belongs to this kinship group by adoption, having received his philosophical education in Germany. Benda's intellectual formation is unambiguously distinct, but it is the more striking, then, that this anti-romantic rationalist should bear a marked resemblance to the others. Only a little biographical licence is needed to advance the historical claim that in this variegated cluster of writings we have so many instances of a single discursive formation, best and most conveniently known as Kulturkritik. The thematic affinities of the group are self-evident: modernity as degeneration, as the valorization of the mass, as the paradoxical hyperactivity of essentially inert forces (the 'revolt' of the 'passive' multitude), as the decay or contamination of traditional, normally minoritarian values, as the disintegrative advance of high and vulgar enlightenment. These are their fixed perceptions, their standard narratives, their shared citations of 'the obvious' – in a phrase, their common sense. Further comparative analysis reveals strict formal identities in their terms of explanation and judgement, and the patterns of their ethico-political desire.

In every case, the object of reflection is a more or less inexorable and co-ordinated historical process. Ortega's name for it is 'capitalism', though his reading stresses its technical rather than its specifically social characteristics. Mannheim's version of 'modern society' acknowledges class conflict (and in this registers an old debt to Marx), but only as a destructive deadlock, a chronic dysfunction without developmental value. Benda offers no articulated account. Mann describes the rise of 'Roman', now French, universalism, with its anti-national norms of humanitarianism, reason and democracy. For Leavis, the most rigorous determinist

of them all, the essential process is that of self-propelled technological advance and its necessary effects, which he summarizes, as
does Mann, in the canonical term 'civilization'. Against this
modern world of meanings, in it but not of it and barely able to
withstand its pressures, are set the antithetical values of spirit.
For Benda, these are the perennial, unqualifiable intellectual goods,
Justice and Truth. For Mann, in a perfect reversal of sensibility,
Kultur is identical with German tradition. Mannheim's vision of
'synthesis' invokes the feudal past while postulating a material
grounding in the future. Ortega's 'culture', unlike Mann's, is
European rather than national. Leavis's is both, playing its critical
part in a theory of industrialism in general but also, and with
ever-strengthening emphasis, signifying the greatness and the
vulnerability of a specifically English moral heritage (Mulhern
[1990] 1998: 133–46).

These constellations of counter-historical value – culture or
spirit – are not merely objects of contemplation in this intellectual tradition. They define the *subject* of Kulturkritik as a discourse. That is, they constitute the position from which the
modern social process is seen, and furnish the terms in which it
must be evaluated, and may perhaps be resisted. In every case,
general contemplation of modernity sustains a more or less tren-
chant ethical discourse on the practice of intellectuals. Each of
these writers insists upon a binary characterology of his own social kind. On the one hand they deplore, with greater or lesser
passion, the works of 'party schools', or the rabble-rousing *laïques*
(the 'lay' intellectual counterparts of the clerisy), or 'the special-
ist', or the enlightened 'literary man', or the academic and
metropolitan racketeer. On the other hand, they insist upon the
duties of the self-consistent 'intellectual', or *le clerc*, or 'the man of
culture', or the inward German artist, or 'the critical minority'.

These professions of faith were in all cases minoritarian. The
course of history seemed irresistible. Pessimism was the characteristic feeling of the texts – not excluding the relatively sanguine

Mannheim's – as they surveyed the repellent evidences of mass society. Yet only Benda counselled withdrawal as a normal response to contemporary disorder, and, even in arguing so, he appealed to assumptions that united him with his most activist counterparts. All five writers concurred in their revulsion from contemporary politics, and in terms that were not themselves politically partisan in any ordinary sense. What Benda stated at the uttermost limit of idealism, the contrastingly worldly Ortega also averred. Modern politics must be rejected not, or not only, because of its current repertoire of options and practices, but because it was intrinsically deficient as a mode of social authority. In Mann's formulation, it was self-contradictory to offer political resistance to civilization, which was, precisely, the triumph of the political mentality as such. As Leavis judged, even the most drastic challenge to the prevailing order – social revolution – was at best 'inessential'. But this repudiation did not entail the abandonment of minority claims to authority. Culture, be it eternal or simply traditional, was an imprescriptible moral reality which might regain at least something of its rightful authority. The images of aristocracy and priesthood that recur in these texts are figures of loss but also of desire – a desire that discovered definite programmatic forms in Mannheim and Leavis, with their parallel visions of an intellectual corporation capable of controlling the blinkered factions that clashed in everyday life. Common topics, common forms of argument, a shared position of vision and address, a single path of ethico-political desire – these are the marks of a strong discursive formation, whose exemplary instance is the discourse of Kulturkritik.

2

IN THE WARS

The will, which Kulturkritik made manifest, to assert the cultural principle as a sovereign social authority, drove successive attempts to move from diagnosis to policy, from witness to action. The earliest and grandest of these was fully official: a League of Nations in culture. In 1922, the League's Council established its Committee on Intellectual Cooperation and, three years later, the Sub-Committee on Arts and Letters – a body including, among others, Thomas Mann. From Paul Valéry, the French representative and poet laureate of European intellectuality between the wars, came the proposal for 'an exchange for literary values', a means whereby the underlying condition of all politics, an idea of 'man and man's duty', could be elucidated by those who specialized in 'values', the intellectuals (Valéry 1963: 69–113). The committee, which was now confirmed as 'permanent', began its work in 1931, organizing an international series of conferences (called *conversations*) and publishing commissioned dialogues on the grave matters of the day (called *correspondances*). Successive conferences probed the future of 'culture' (1933) and 'the European mind' (also 1933), or projected 'a new humanism' (1936). The *correspondances* series included, among other things, an exchange of letters between Sigmund Freud and Albert Einstein, *Why War?* (published in 1932, Freud 1985: 341–62).

Ortega's initiative was more confined in scale, but, if anything, more practical in intent. In 1931, he entered the parliament of the new Spanish republic as part of the Agrupación al Servício de la República, the collective 'man of culture' in political form (Preston 1987: 89). Mannheim, thwarted by the triumph of German fascism, fled to Britain and there, in the later 1930s, launched a second attempt to nurture his 'forum' into practical being. In 1938, the Church of England's Christian Council on Faith and the Common Life created the Moot, something like a national version of Valéry's 'exchange', involving intellectuals in seminars and publishing ventures designed to bring their corporate wisdom to bear on the modern crisis, to saturate politics with thought (Kojecký 1971: 163–97; Steele 1997: 98–117). For as long as the Moot existed, Mannheim was at the centre of its work, elaborating his vision of a planned society led by educated elites. Among the participants in Moot events were collaborators in Leavis's *Scrutiny*, which made its own contribution to this group of initiatives by calling for a 'movement in education'. Propagating the journal's diagnosis of mass civilization in the classroom, and equipping a new generation with the intellectual means to resist the machine in society at large, this movement would constitute the distinctive 'politics' of English Kulturkritik (Mulhern 1979: 107f).

None of these initiatives proved sustainable, let alone effective. Valéry's exchange did not outlive its equally abstracted sponsoring body; the last conference gathered in Nice in 1938 to 'plan' a future that was already being settled by military force. The *conversations* and *correspondances* were aptly styled – genres of personal intercourse, not public engagement. The short life of the Agrupación (1931–3) cast doubt on the ability of the cultural interest to turn shared intuition into cohesive political practice. Ortega, who had been elected with socialist support, employed himself in stock anti-socialist tirades in the Madrid parliament. His fellow-men of culture dispersed to various political quarters, becoming Radicals, independent centrists or activists in the proto-fascist Frente Español. The Moot, rather farther removed from presumptions of influence and from the centres of political crisis, survived beyond the Second World War, but was so little fuelled by collective passion that it died with its inspirational figure. A 'forum' indeed, the Moot was always politically miscellaneous, placid in the manner of its Anglican sponsor, embracing several varieties of conservative, liberal and socialist. Of its literary remains, the best known is T.S. Eliot's *Notes Towards the Definition of Culture* ([1948] 1962), a work which, ironically, dedicated itself to refuting Mannheimian and kindred visions of culture and society. Leavis's 'movement in education' was, in its way, more successful than any of its cognates. His practical scheme for the institutional ascendancy of English literary studies, although coming to nothing as policy, served as a pattern of individual mission for a generation of teachers. But that was the limit of achievement. This was a self-styled movement without organization or instruments, in which the banner of 'politics' was raised as a sign of culture's practical intent, but not much more.

Endeavours such as these were the means by which Kulturkritik thought to defend its intuitions of continuity, order, wholeness and humanity, and so far as possible, to discover an authoritative social role for itself in the anarchic conditions of modernity. The resistance they faced was, of course, that of the social order itself, in its typical, spontaneous manifestations: the blind momentum of industrial economies, the clamour of hustings and markets, the presumption of the masses and the cynicism of their mock-intellectual flatterers. It was after all in naming such menaces that Kulturkritik identified and justified the corporate function of intelligence, its special role in the life of the social 'body'. However, challenges of another kind came from within that putative corporation, in the writings of theorists and critics for whom the high tradition of culture, with its familiar repertoire of questions and answers, was not the self-validating ground of right judgement but a curiosity in itself.

FREUD'S CRITIQUE OF KULTUR

Sigmund Freud's official contribution to the intellectuals' politics of inter-war Europe was as one great thinker in dialogue with another concerning the phenomenon of human aggression – an exercise he privately thought tiresome and pointless (Freud 1985: 344). His independently-motivated intervention in this arena – for *Civilization and Its Discontents*, together with its companion-piece, *The Future of an Illusion* (dating from 1930 and 1927, respectively), may be seen as such – was, in its basic principle, a rejection of such high-minded pieties. Citing the canonical opposition of 'culture' and 'civilization', Freud declared: 'I scorn to distinguish between [them]' (1985: 184). This was in one respect a moral gesture, resonant in its time and place. Thomas Mann was one of many to have invoked those terms in affirming Germanic spiritual uniqueness – and indeed Freud's original title referenced the crucial *Kultur*, and not 'civilization', which, perhaps in the same irreverent spirit, he recommended for the English translation (p. 182). The gesture was justified also on theoretical grounds, depending as it did on the thesis by which psychoanalysis asserted its explanatory claims in the field of the social sciences. Freud proposed a monist interpretation of all mental life. Call it culture or call it civilization, learned social behaviour formed a single complex shaped by the necessities of the human constitution. Culture–civilization was the mode in which human animals adapted their instincts for the purposes of coexistence. The practices and institutions so characterized might be valued as progressive developments from a natural state, or, in an older tradition, as manifestations of another, contrastingly spiritual order of being. In fact, they were functional modifications of a changeless human condition. 'Repression' and 'sublimation' were the constitutive processes through which society's sanctioned meanings and values were constituted. The erotic and aggressive drives must be inhibited as, for example, in legal and ethical codes, or, in a complementary process, rendered 'sublime', directed towards substitute, idealized satisfactions in the 'higher' pursuits of truth and beauty. The work of culture–civilization was thus both controlling and formative. Its means included, as well as dictates and prohibitions, the canonized arts of mind and body – philosophy, poetry, music, dance. Yet culture remained an activity of restless animals, not a privileged realm apart. Contrary to a whole tradition of aesthetic education, it was not a means to an attainable human completeness and fulfilment, but the creation of self-division, frustration and guilt – a promise of happiness, perhaps, but, inevitably, a false one.

As psychoanalysis, *Civilization and Its Discontents* (Freud [1930] 1985) set out a mordant commentary on the spiritual pretensions of culture and its intellectual representatives. The pronounced iconoclasm of tone (which illustrated Freud's theory, suggesting something of the sadistic gratifications of critical thought) signified deliberate polemical intent. Indeed, it would have been possible to press further, to interpret the characteristic social phobias of Kulturkritik as cases of projection, symptoms of the unavowable knowledge that 'civilization' is one and the same as the 'culture' that fends it off. As Theodor Adorno observed, some twenty years later, in an unmistakable allusion to Freud, 'the cultural critic is not happy with civilization, to which alone he owes his discontent. ... Yet he is necessarily of the same essence as that to which he fancies himself superior' (Adorno [1955] 1981: 19). However, psychoanalytic reason did not operate alone in Freud's anthropology. In extending his core theory into the field of collective life, he took two risks. In one movement of thought, he constructed human history as a great biography, refiguring the entire species as a collective individual. At the same time, he assimilated, as if by default, the dominant social discourse of his day, simply rewriting it in the language of psychoanalysis.

Freud's title, *Civilization and Its Discontents*, was something of a misnomer. His grounding conceptual distinction is between the individual and the social, and there is no real parity between them ([1930] 1985: 284–5). The literal individual, the organic singularity, is explored with all the accumulated theoretical resources of psychoanalysis, which at the same time sustain the metaphor of the species–individual. But, except in this questionable extrapolation, the category of 'civilization', the social, remains unspecified. For Freud, as for the liberal tradition, the individual was the full category, the source of energy, desire and purposes. Society is its supplement, the mere framework of protection and restraint. A few perfunctory references to work, technology, science and law, abstracted from the historical systems of production and power that organize them, serve as an account of the social order. His passing comments on communism and socialism were measured in a way that suggested educated politeness rather than critical openness (pp. 303, 305–6). Proffered in the name of unblinking scientific realism, his major social-anthropological claims rehearsed a commonplace mock-aristocratic pessimism. 'The common man' and 'individuals of the leader type', 'weaklings' and 'stronger natures' marked the poles of his social imagination (pp. 261, 294–5, 307). 'Masses are lazy and unintelligent', he wrote in *The Future of an Illusion*, 'they have no love for instinctual renunciation, and they are not to be convinced by argument of its inevitability; and the individuals composing them support one another in giving free rein to their indiscipline' (Freud [1927] 1985: 186).

Progress in renunciation was conceivable, Freud allowed, though it would be limited and vulnerable. The 'superior, unswerving, disinterested' minority could scarcely hope to win general authority for their insights by education alone, but would have to deploy 'means to power', 'a certain degree of coercion', in the pursuit of civilized unhappiness for all. Or in the watchword of Matthew

Arnold, the lawgiver of English liberal education, who affirmed that culture might hope to tame anarchy but must not in any case tolerate it: 'force till right is ready' (Arnold [1864] 1964: 16).

Freud's theoretical renunciation of Kulturkritik, his 'scorn' for the pretensions of cultural spirituality, entailed its own kind of self-destruction. It was, in a strict sense, tragic. He demonstrated, from his own theoretical premises, the substantial unity of 'culture' and 'civilization', and thereby undermined the rationale of 'the man of culture'. However, lacking any comparable access to critical concepts of specifically social-historical reference, he was unable to account for the prevailing social order of culture. Acting on his radical insights into the nature of the human animal, yet held in the conventions of a traditional, pre-democratic authoritarian liberalism, he saw in contemporary social relations only the probably inescapable forms and predicaments of a second nature. A few superior, unswerving, disinterested beings, and, swarming around them, the lazy, unintelligent masses. This was the world according to Kulturkritik.

WOOLF'S ANDROGYNY

For any who cared to inspect the less anxious varieties of this discourse – not so much Kulturkritik as a display of cultivated self-regard – there was no need to look beyond the environs of Freud's English publisher, the Hogarth Press, in the central London district called Bloomsbury. Virginia Woolf was Hogarth's principal author and, with her husband, Leonard, its proprietor. Their home was a venue for one of the most remarkable formations of the earlier twentieth century in England – a circle including the novelist E.M. Forster, Virginia's sister, the painter Vanessa Bell, and the economist John Maynard Keynes. The Bloomsbury Group, as it came to be called, characteristically disclaimed the strong common identity this given name implied. They were simply a network of 'friends'. Yet in *Civilization* (Bell 1928),

Vanessa's husband Clive offered something like a manifesto. The vestige of a much larger work, now abandoned, to have been called *The New Renaissance*, Bell's essay yielded none of its morale in the face of this evidence of blockage. Civilization, the general condition favouring the experience of 'good states of mind', was the work of the civilized and civilizing few, he maintained. It depended on the existence of a leisured class, and, supporting that, a labouring population secure enough to benefit from the civilizing process. The class struggle between capital and labour was a contention of philistines, and could not, in any of its outcomes, establish this necessary social foundation. A co-ordinated strategy of economic and demographic development, including technological innovation and, for the unassimilable labour surplus, policies of selective breeding and planned emigration were the means by which a civilized future would come about. It is as well to say at this point that 'civilization', in Bloomsbury parlance, was a positive value.

Bell's book opened with a dedicatory letter to Virginia Woolf, who, in an essay written perhaps not much later, refigured her brother-in-law's happy sociology in the standard phrenological metaphor of the day, the intellectual hierarchy of 'brows' (Bell 1928: v–viii; Woolf 1942).[1] Woolf's purpose was to affirm the integrity and mutuality of 'highbrow' and 'lowbrow' as cultural types, in the face of an intruding third type, the 'middlebrow'. A highbrow like herself was 'the man or woman of thoroughbred intelligence who rides his mind at a gallop across country in pursuit of an idea' (Woolf 1942: 147). A lowbrow, 'of course', was someone of 'thoroughbred vitality who rides his body in pursuit of a living at a gallop across life'. Highbrows 'needed' and 'honoured' lowbrows, each group finding in the other the indispensable complement of their own genius, which was for 'life', or for reflection upon it, but never both. Woolf pointedly distinguished her cultural taxonomy from the existing order of social classes – a standard disclaimer in this discursive tradition – and, although that unwelcome association returned in the opposition of 'country', the real property across which the highbrow rides, and 'life', the notional acreage of one's own person, which was the lowbrow's allotted space, there was indeed something not merely social in its construction. It was, as her phrenological and pastoral imagery confirmed, the natural, fecund order of things. But the middlebrows would not understand this. Seeking to represent themselves as the cultural equals of highbrows, they achieved only the deathly mannerism of good taste. Seeking to redeem lowbrows from the neglect of precious elites, 'to teach them culture', they patronized them and subjected their spontaneous beauty of expression to jejune schemes of improvement (p. 152). In what some might think of as education, Woolf saw the making of monsters. These 'go-betweens', these 'busybodies', were sterile hybrids, Woolf declared, offences against cultural nature. Their ambitions were hardly less absurd than the fantasy of transcending 'husbands and wives' and creating 'a middle sex' (p. 154).

This essay showed Woolf in her most complacent aspect, devising, as if for a weekend entertainment, a peculiarly fatalistic variation on the topic of minority culture, its natural privileges and the unnatural latter-day encroachments upon them. However, Woolf's writing was discursively complex, here assuming one perspective and voice, elsewhere seeing and speaking quite otherwise. She proved capable on another occasion – in her 'Memories of a Working Women's Guild' – of a far more self-critical appreciation of initiatives in popular self-education (1967: 134–48); and she was capable also of the most searching critique of her highbrow cultural inheritance. Freud, in *Civilization and Its Discontents*, demystified the spiritualizing self-consciousness of Kultur, elucidating the psycho-biological drives that shaped and powered it. Yet in as much as a strong concept of human nature remained central to his account, although now in a materialist form, he spared the humanistic claim to general validity and authority. In *A Room of One's Own* ([1929] 1977), Woolf deployed a specifically social materialism against traditional notions of cultural unity and universality.

This short book famously, controversially, availed itself of 'all the liberties and licences of a novelist' (p. 6). Yet, however much or little fictional play may have gone into them, the reminiscences and conjectures of the first three chapters supported a single polemical thesis: culture, supposedly a general, inclusively human good, has been formed under 'the rule of a patriarchy'. The foundations of this rule are 'grossly material'. Woolf described the real and also symbolic limitations on women's access to the means of learning and thought. She identified the old male usurpation of women's rights in property and income as the enabling condition of women's intellectual and artistic marginality, and went on to show how, even in reformed circumstances, that hereditary impoverishment must limit women's efforts on their own behalf. Culture, as actually formed, was not merely characterized by the unequal appropriation of common values. On the contrary, the dominant values were themselves gendered in their deep constitution. This was an order of representation in which women were compulsively, often angrily discoursed upon by men, more, it would seem, than any other 'animal in the universe' (p. 27); one in which habitual symbolic elevation transfigured the realities of subordination and marginality. Even where this male-centred culture enabled specific innovations on women's part, it left them awkward and alone before a repertoire of styles and topics that was common, and thus authoritative, yet not common at all, having taken shape in a world dominated by men and largely reserved to them. Tested against the reality of such practical and psychic confinement, the idea of irrepressible genius was an illusion. Judith Shakespeare, had she lived and followed her brother's path, could only have died wretchedly.

What, then, might be the conditions of women's deliverance from this objective and subjective system of oppression? Woolf proposed a means and a goal. In keeping with her insistent materialism

– which, in striking contrast with the habit of Kulturkritik, emphasized property and attendant inequalities rather than the supposedly degraded equality of the market place – she maintained that for women, as for any social category, the prerequisites of creativity were strictly practical in kind. The historical pattern of women's artistic creativity confirmed so much, showing more strongly in areas where the means of production were cheap and unobtrusive (say, pen and paper) but little or not at all where more costly and imposing instruments were called for. Material access and control were the conditions of women's emergence as autonomous cultural producers – or, in the famous synecdoche, 'money and a room of her own' (p. 6). These basic gains would enable women writers to commence a long, collective journey towards emancipation from an oppressively gendered culture. Woolf refused to accept that progress in this could be measured against fixed evaluative norms. Prevailing intuitions of quality and capacity were stylizations of a history of ignorance and oppression, and to defer to them would be 'abject treachery'. She envisioned a process both radical and awkward, that would change all the familiar terms of writing and representation, and whose deepest sense would be a release into free and full subjective life. The prevailing order of gender was not simply discriminatory. It denied the innate bisexuality of the human psyche, and confined all subjectivity to a narrow binary scheme of dispositions and performances – the stereotyped routines of masculinity-or-femininity. Women and men were all, in truth, 'woman–manly' and 'man–womanly' in varying degrees, and the leitmotiv of an emancipated culture would be uninhibited embrace of this reality, in the moral-stylistic value of 'androgyny'.[2]

This is the leading tendency in the reasoning of *A Room of One's Own*, and, in a strict feminist sense (though Woolf held that appellation at a distance), it is revolutionary. But it progresses in the face of a counter-tendency, whose effects contribute equally to the pattern of the text, revealing a bifocal vision of culture, a doubleness of discursive position. The crux of the book, as has often been said, is 'anger'. Woolf condemned the defensive chauvinist anger of a patriarchal culture, and found reason in the angers of the women it subordinated, her own included. Yet, she insisted that anger had no place in art, whose highest achievements, indeed, were distinguished by the transcendence of such 'alien' feeling. She deplored the effects of its intrusion into a work such as *Jane Eyre*. Commenting on Charlotte Brontë's novel, she wrote:

> the woman who wrote those pages had more genius in her than Jane Austen; but if one reads them over and marks that jerk in them, that indignation, one sees that she will never get her genius expressed whole and entire. She will write in a rage where she should write calmly. She will write foolishly where she should write wisely. ... She is at war with her lot.
>
> (Woolf [1929] 1977: 66–7)

This is a perplexing turn in a work of feminist criticism, and a paradoxical judgement from the woman who could muster the rhetorical force of those sentences: here, as Woolf wrote of Brontë, 'the continuity is disturbed'. The female 'sex-consciousness' without which there could not have been *A Room of One's Own* emerges as the enemy of women's creative fulfilment.

Matters of tactics and personal disposition played a part in the shaping of this crux, but to dwell upon them is merely to displace the problem, which is fundamental, amounting to self-contradiction. This logical difficulty marks a fault-line in the discursive constitution of Woolf's reasoning, and finds a revealing parallel in the historical perspectives she adopts. In fact, *A Room of One's Own* proposes two discrepant historical narratives. One is long, continuous and unfinished, that of an oppression traced back through the centuries of English literature into an unmeasured past. The other is short, coextensive with Woolf's lifetime, and is broken in two. The signature of the later and darker phase was the intensified 'sex-consciousness' of both women and men, in whom, Woolf believed, there existed a masculinist state of emergency provoked 'no doubt' by the campaign for women's suffrage. Against her observations of this phase, she set the reverie of a lighter, more youthful and various style of inter-sexual exchange, which she gave as a memory of Oxbridge before the war (pp. 13–16) – the kind of memory which, as it happened, Clive Bell had already suggested to her in the dedicatory address of his *Civilization* (Bell 1928: v). These rival histories belong to rival discourses. The first and more powerful of the two is plainly feminist, defined by the opposition between a patriarchal order and women's resistance to it. In the second, that opposition is displaced by another, between art, and the civilizing relations it nourishes, and politics, the racking, disfiguring antagonisms of a divided society.

Viewed in this light, the notion of androgyny served not one purpose but two. It is the equivocal image that assuages the discursive self-division of Woolf's text. In one of its meanings, androgyny is utopian, the defining quality of a future liberation from oppressive gender relations. But that condition, for Woolf, has less to do with variousness than with plenitude. Its glosses are unity, wholeness, integration and resolution, which are, as Woolf believed, the proper attributes of art and literature as such.[3] Utopian imagining commonly draws its inspiration from the past. But here is a utopia whose foreshadowings were already official monuments. It was Coleridge who formulated the notion of creative androgyny. Shakespeare and Austen were its exemplary incarnations. Even the tragic Judith, who figures the damage of the past but also the promise of a better day, was not just anyone's sister. Elaborated in this way, androgyny discloses its second, not at all subversive, aspect. In this meaning, which neutralizes the critical charge of the first, the notion of androgyny works to redeem the received canon of cultural value from patriarchal deformation and to reinstate it as a judgement on the present and a norm for the future.[4] Here, Woolf discloses her spiritual kinship with Matthew Arnold. Arnold's cultural criticism, which Leavis directly continued, entailed a strategic distinction between the 'best self', in which a whole and 'disinterested' humanity was present and active, and the 'ordinary self', in which particular and therefore antagonistic social interests predominated (Arnold [1869] 1932). Woolfian androgyny differs from the disinterested best self in its sensuous psychic texturing, but its parallel critical function, recognizable from Leavis's Kulturkritik, is to validate a superordinate cultural wholeness, an authority fit to regulate the blind factionalism of mere politics, including 'sex consciousness'. Thus, the figure of androgyny both crowned Woolf's feminism and capped it. She exposed the false, patriarchal universalism of the dominant culture and, in the same rhetorical gesture, exonerated it, reimagining custom, the custom of her own class fraction, as liberation.[5]

ORWELL'S ENGLISH

In the earliest of Bloomsbury's studies in cultural sociology – this one a novel, *Howards End* (1910) – E.M. Forster entertained the contrast between the 'civilized', free-thinking Schlegels and the philistine Wilcoxes, but then displaced it, showing how English leisure-class cultivation, the life of the mind, depended upon the entrepreneurs and administrators of the Imperial economy, whose profits sustained the miracle of civilization. He also showed how these two bourgeois types, for all the conventional antipathy between them, had far more disturbing social others in common: the aspirational middlebrow Bast, his coarse wife, Jackie, and, in the darkness below them, the unrepresentable proletariat for whom they did symbolic service. Eric Blair grew into the role of a lesser Wilcox, but then remade himself as a writer, George Orwell, who would enter the moral and symbolic world of those social others, and discover in it a judgement on the Schlegels of his own day. In this sense, his work constituted a polemical inversion of the perceptual and evaluative scheme of Kulturkritik.

'What is strange about these people is their invisibility.' Orwell was writing on this occasion about the labouring poor of Marrakesh, and more generally about 'people with brown skins' (Orwell 1961: 391–2). In another context – his long essay on Charles Dickens – he extended his observation to include the English working class, though now with the crucial suggestion that this 'strangeness' was conventional: not a variety of being but the effect of prevailing norms of literary representation and the social valuations they confirmed. The motif of travel and discovery that dominates so much of Orwell's work is, then, ethical and political in function. The will to revelation is also a commitment to exposure and rebuke. His writing does not merely report a certain state of affairs: its characteristic purpose is to specify and correct or attack the cultural conditions that make reporting necessary, the conditions of obscurity. In keeping with this, his writing on literature and other cultural forms, though always emphasizing political values, is formalist and sociological in its procedures. It is a deliberate and self-conscious mode of inquiry rather than another variety of moral exertion. Thus, Orwell reads Dickens's narratives as instances of a quite regular cosmology of Victorian capitalism: a specific construction and evaluation of its system of classes and a determinate array of probable and desirable outcomes. The forms of the fiction, here as in any case, are in and of themselves its politics, and may appropriately be judged in such terms. The pleasures they afford or inhibit are, by the same token, a mode of moral experience, and can be explored as evidence of the dispositions of their readers (1961: 413–60).

'Charles Dickens' remained, if only by virtue of its subject, a study in literary criticism. In 'Boys' Weeklies' and 'The Art of Donald McGill', two essays written in the same phase of his career, Orwell left home yet again, entering the other world of popular pleasure and the uncreated discourse of cultural studies. Both essays opened, appropriately, with the gesture of introduction: they would deal not with familiar matters of educated interest but with the obscure or despised objects of majority pleasure. Moreover, they would study these objects – comic magazines and postcards – to discover their meaning, not to confirm the lack of it. Orwell gave detailed descriptions of his materials, sorting them by genre, convention and topic. The representations of nationality, race and class, in the darkening conditions of the thirties, dominated the analysis of comics. The imagery of sexuality, gender and marriage was the inevitable issue in the study of McGill's bawdy narrative cartoons. In both cases, the ultimate goal of understanding lay beyond the texts themselves, in their popular audiences.

Periodical papers offered a fine gauge of popular inclinations, Orwell maintained, because unlike cinema and radio programmes, they were in some meaningful degree chosen by their users. The local newsagent's display gave 'the best available indication' of what 'the mass of the English people really feels and thinks' (1961: 461). The sheer ubiquity of McGill's postcards seemed proof of their interpretive value. No practitioner of Kulturkritik would have disagreed, but Orwell's evaluative presumption, unthinkable in that tradition, was that popular culture might educate the educators. In boys' weeklies he discerned, amid all the reactionary celebrations of the British Imperial homeland, a 'family' patriotism that would not be denied. In McGill's cards, with their fearsome wives, big-bosomed temptresses and puny, luckless men, Orwell traced the stoical sexual imagination of the popular classes – the narratives of desire and frustration they expect as naturally theirs – but also the signs of an inexhaustible spirit of defiance. These cards were part of that 'chorus of raspberries' with which 'the millions of common men' responded to the 'high sentiments' of official England. 'Like the music halls, they are a sort of saturnalia, a harmless rebellion against virtue' (Orwell 1970a: 194).

The popular culture Orwell explored was that of an exploitative class order. His evaluation of it was grounded in his position on the left. However, his understanding of that order and his relationship with such politics were radically ambivalent. Writing in 1941, he declared flatly that war had exposed the bankruptcy of capitalism, and argued that only socialist revolution could secure the conditions of a successful military effort. Yet in the same text, *The Lion and the Unicorn*, he dismissed the 'doctrine of the class war' as an 'out-of-date gospel', and characterized England as 'a family with the wrong members in control' (1970a: 92, 68). Indeed, Orwell seemed often to observe a law of inverse proportion such that the more fiercely he insisted upon class realities the more he trivialized them: 'England is the most class-ridden country under the sun', he wrote. It 'resembles ... a rather stuffy Victorian family', one in which 'the young are generally thwarted and most of the power is in the hands of irresponsible uncles and bed-ridden aunts' (pp. 67–8). On another occasion, he traced the cultural apartheid of the middle class to their disgust at bad smells, and beckoned them towards socialism with the assurance that 'we have nothing to lose but our aitches' (1970d). Here, likewise, was a declared socialist in whose writing the principal genre was exasperated, often hostile dialogue with the left in general. Although the second part of *The Road to Wigan Pier* looked towards a socialism that could put an end to the social wretchedness depicted in the first, its best-known passages are those composed in ridicule of fellow-socialists. The studies in popular culture were similarly constructed. Generals, popes, dictators, temperance campaigners but also 'left-wing political parties' appeared in random sequence in Orwell's list of the pious authorities to whom McGill's carnivalesque audience would never quite submit (1970a: 193). 'Boys' Weeklies' turned on a critical motif that would one day become the call-sign of studies in popular culture: the left's 'failure to understand'. What the left failed to understand on this early occasion was the reality of England's 'family' patriotism, against which callow internationalism would never prevail. The evidence was available in 'popular imaginative literature', but this was 'a field that left-wing thought has never begun to enter' (1961: 484). The work of Rudyard Kipling, rather higher in register but still popular, might raise 'a snigger in pansy-left circles', Orwell wrote around the same time. But he possessed a sense of responsibility, and, unlike 'the middle-class left', whose political avowals were in any case 'a sham', he perceived 'very clearly that men can only be highly civilized while other men, inevitably less civilized, are there to guard and feed them' (1970a: 215–29).

Case-by-case discrimination of such moments, which the essayistic character of Orwell's work encourages, and which for certain purposes is necessary, should not distract attention from the fact that they are normal features of his writing: that they define its identity and orientation in the politics of culture. The contraries of class and politics that dominated these studies in popular culture, as they would wholly absorb his late novels, were themselves subject to a more fundamental binary. In committing himself to 'the working masses who make up seventy-five per cent of the population', Orwell was not merely, or even principally, aligning his social purposes with those of the exploited classes, for in his moral sociology those masses were, in truth, the nation itself, 'the English people proper' (1970b: 10). And 'the left', correspondingly, became something less, or other, than the collective herald of socialism. 'There is now no intelligentsia that is not in some sense "left"', Orwell wrote, in one of those false generalizations for which he came to be revered, and in his own terms the proposition bore a necessary truth. For just as the working class was the contemporary mode of being of England's 'common people', so the left was the current behavioural mode of an alien cultural category, the intellectuals. These twin identifications determined the character of Orwell's discourse on culture. In the aesthetic and recreational preferences of the social majority, he discerned the imperishable moral strengths of a people. While in the typical dispositions of the intelligentsia, there was little but ignorance, conformism, and nihilism mounting to treachery.

The negative imagery of Kulturkritik, which Orwell largely dis-
allowed as a valid representation of the common life, was retained
and intensified to the level of compulsive, phobic abuse in his
characterizations of its cultural others. 'Pansy' leftists, 'nancy
poets', 'flabbily', 'squashily' pacifist, bigoted votaries of the 'ruth-
less ideologies of the continent' who 'snigger at every English institution' – 'if the 'intellectuals' had done their work a little more
thoroughly, Britain would have surrendered in 1940' (1970a:
74–5; 1970b: 111, 106, 332–41). Such words speak for, and
against, themselves.

Orwell saw in the political waywardness of the intelligentsia
the index of its alienation from 'the common people'. The structural condition of this divorce was 'the anachronistic class system', which must be ended politically, through a popular
reconstruction of the nation. The specifically cultural effect of intellectual alienation was evident in the body of the English language itself, which had:

> grown anaemic because for long past it has not been invigo-
> rated from below. ... Language ought to be the joint creation of
> poets and manual workers, and in modern England it is diffi-
> cult for these two classes to meet. When they do so again – as,
> in a different way, they could in the feudal past – English may
> show more clearly than at present its kinship with the lan-
> guage of Shakespeare and Defoe.
>
> (Orwell 1970b: 29)

But for now, there was the linguistic 'decadence' that was perhaps
Orwell's most sustained cultural interest in his last ten years. The
linguistic commentaries he wrote in the 1940s bear a recognizable affinity with the philological moralism that was one of the
traditions of Kulturkritik. The American H.L. Mencken and the
Austrian Karl Kraus were legendary practitioners of the genre,
also as journalists (Mencken [1919] 1936; Kraus 1984); and in England, the *Scrutiny* group also upheld the language of Shakespeare as

the bench-mark by which modern decadence might be judged. But the comparison is one of kind, not achievement, for Orwell's critical faculties were seldom exercised with less discipline than in this field. He favoured a deliberate programme of neologism, yet he also repudiated the metric system on the grounds that grammes and litres could never achieve the idiomatic resonance of 'homely' ounces and inches (1970b: 3–12; 1970c: 306). The judgements of the celebrated late essay 'Politics and the English Language' (1946) – in favour of gerunds, against double negatives, and so on – were facile or downright crass (1970c: 156–70). What these and other essays do show is that, for Orwell, the condition of English was of crucial cultural interest, and the nature of that interest is best seen not so much in the themes of his linguistic commentaries as in the language he fashioned as his own means of analysis, judgement and self-definition.

'Plain' is one of the epithets conventionally attached to Orwell's prose, but the sense of that description is itself far from plain. Perhaps the most nearly plain varieties of language use are jargons, more or less technical codes developed for the specified purposes of elective user communities. And in this sense, 'plainness' in non-technical utterance is also coded: it is an effect of a jargon that cannot know itself as such, the jargon of familiarity. Familiarities are always historically determinate, involving specific social affinities and a correspondingly specific 'common sense'. To idealize a social jargon as 'plain' is to enforce its underlying values as the cultural norm. However, the familiarity that Orwell valued was, precisely, not available as a formed language variety: the creative union of poets and manual workers was no more than a possibility on the far side of revolution. His style was a utopian attempt to embody that imaginable social familiarity, to anticipate its redemptive cultural authority in the forms of language – with effects that were not, in any simple descriptive sense, plain. Discontinuity of register is among its most regular features. The main register is that of informal educated speech. The syntax is orthodox, though tending to avoid more complex constructions, and the effort to avoid cultivated ceremony is marked by the use of *you*, not *one*, as the impersonal pronoun, and of the contracted form of the negative (*didn't* rather than *did not*). But this register is again and again disturbed by others, sometimes learned but normally more colloquial. The use of *stuff* as a synonym for writing (which Virginia Woolf accurately diagnosed as a mark of the no-nonsense middlebrow) is a case of this, as is the wilfully indiscriminate use, in the essay on Dickens, of *idiocy* as a term of condemnation. The closing sentence of the same essay, with its denunciation of 'the smelly little orthodoxies ... now contending for our souls', illustrates the imagery of physical disgust, often homophobic in character, to which Orwell's prose is so systematically given: *squashy*, *flabby*, *pansy*, *nancy*, the abusive animal metaphors of *The Road to Wigan Pier*.

Such disruptions of register, which are not 'plain' but rather a baroque impersonation of 'plain speaking', testify to the crisis-ridden desire of Orwell's cultural criticism. He looked beyond the contraries of highbrow and masses towards an authentically national popular culture, and strained to image it in a normative English prose style. But in doing so, he violently disavowed his own status as an intellectual, and travestied popularity by recourse to a diction whose educated origins in schoolboy argot were manifest. The dream of a culture at once common and authoritative produced a language prone to coarseness and intimidation. Orwell's whole effort, in his writing on culture, was to strike beyond the discursive borders of Kulturkritik; his language is the monument to his failure.

MARXIST INCURSIONS

Freud's psychoanalysis exposed the dualism of Kulturkritik, but in a social perspective that reproduced its minoritarian – aristocratic – fatalism. Woolf's feminism exposed the oppressive gen-

dering of the dominant cultural universalism and looked beyond
it to an emancipated androgyny – which, however, also restored the
lineage she had threatened to dispossess. Orwell's anti-imperialism,
developing into socialism, led him to invert the customary soli-
darities of Kulturkritik, to validate the desires and capacities of
the popular underworld, but in the mode of national romance – a
personal utopia equivalent to Woolf's androgyny – that, as in the
less complex instances of Mann and Leavis, was itself a variety of
Kulturkritik. Although all these challenges had deadly critical
potential, none escaped the gravitational field of that inherited
discourse.

Marxist theory, in the same years, posed more radical challenges to it. Like Freud, the English theorist Christopher
Caudwell declined to honour the spiritualizing claims of Kultur,
in which he saw one manifestation among others of the developing relationship between the human organism and its environment.
In contrast with psychoanalysis, however, Caudwell's conception
of that relationship was historical. The fundamental structure in
which 'man' engaged with 'nature' was the economy, whose successive forms were therefore the expressive heart of all social and
cultural convention. 'Modern poetry', he wrote, 'is *capitalist* poetry'
(Caudwell 1937). As such, it was self-doomed. All Caudwell's
critical studies – a prodigious body of work encompassing literature and science, philosophy, psychology and social theory, as well
as stock themes such as love and beauty – reiterated a single critical thesis. Modern culture as a whole, he maintained, was in the
grip of an 'illusion', the constitutive illusion of capitalist property, that 'freedom' was the negation of social relations, that the
human reality of 'the individual' could find full expression only
outside collective bonds. Freud's psychology, Lawrence's novels,
the avant-garde art of the Surrealists, contemporary trends in theoretical physics all testified, under Caudwell's judicial gaze, to
'the bourgeois illusion' at the heart of capitalism's 'dying culture'
(Caudwell [1938 and 1949] 1971).

Caudwell discerned the imprint of capitalism in even the most rarefied or intimate particulars of cultural life. In this, his critical endeavour matched that of the German Marxist Herbert Marcuse. The greater strength of Marcuse's contemporaneous intervention in this field was that it used a generalized representation of capitalism to ground the analysis of a correspondingly general cultural object, which was not, as in Caudwell's case, a given corpus of literature and thought, but the meta-discourse that regulated all literary and intellectual practice, the discourse of the cultural principle itself (Marcuse [1937] 1972: 88–133). The idea of culture in this sense subsumed the ancient distinction between the 'liberal' and the 'useful' or 'servile' arts: on the one hand, the specifically human pursuit of truth, beauty and virtue, the proper attachments of free persons, but, on the other hand, the skills that bounded the possibilities of the great majority, whose lives must be dominated by narrow toil. In the labour-intensive slave economy of Antiquity, this ordering of things was necessary and morally self-confirming. However, Marcuse argued, it could not survive unchanged in the bourgeois era, which promoted quite distinct relations of property and labour, and more inclusive notions of human identity and possibility. Thus, in the new class order, the liberal pursuits of the few came to be refigured as the integrally human domain of culture – which, however, now came to be seen in abstraction from ordinary social relations. Culture now figured as a redemptive space in which the narrowness, division, inequality and suffering of the social order were annulled, a place where existence achieved wholeness and composure. But this was 'a promise of happiness' that could not be kept, other than in the mode of 'inwardness', in the nurturing of individual sensibility.[6] It gave contemplative access to what bourgeois society could not yield in fact. 'Culture' was thus 'affirmative' in the worse as well as the better sense of the word: the vicarious experience of freedom mediated resignation and conformism, and in this way served the purposes of oppression. Indeed, culture so conceived was the mark of social oppression, Marcuse reasoned, and would persist along with it. The moment of real emancipation, the final calling in of the promise of happiness, would be its vanishing point.

The received value of 'culture' could have no place in Caudwell's psycho-historical materialist scheme. Marcuse sought to elicit the dialectic of its emergence and functioning in bourgeois society. Another German Marxist, Walter Benjamin, more political than either in critical style, disrupted the conceptual identity of Kulturkritik, in effect setting it against itself. In Benjamin's usage, the familiar appeal to 'tradition' became crucially self-aware. It was not, now, a body of values to be defended against the consuming advance of modernity, but a way of intervening in the historical process, a form of the politics that would determine its uncertain social outcome. The past was a theatre in the struggle for the future. 'Historical materialism', he wrote, in his late 'Theses on the Philosophy of History':

> wishes to retain that image of the past which unexpectedly appears to man singled out by history at a moment of danger. The danger affects both the content of the tradition and its receivers. The same threat hangs over both: that of becoming a tool of the ruling classes. In every era the attempt must be made anew to wrest tradition away from a conformism that is about to overpower it. ... Only that historian will have the gift of fanning the spark of hope in the past who is firmly convinced that *even the dead* will not be safe from the enemy if he wins. And this enemy has not ceased to be victorious.
>
> (Benjamin [1940] 1970: 257)

Technology, the engine of historical destruction in the world of Kulturkritik, was revalued by Benjamin in the same revolutionary spirit, becoming a force for cultural emancipation. In the cinema, as technical apparatus and social institution, he discerned the emergence of a newly analytic mode of artistic production and a newly critical, 'expert' audience ([1936] 1970: 219–53). The epochal significance of film, for him, was its mechanical reproducibility, and specifically its status as an art practice that superseded the distinction between original and copy. As such, it heralded the dissolution of 'the aura', the mysterious power associated with the physically 'unique' work of art. Post-auratic art could not claim or be accorded that irrational privilege, Benjamin believed; it belonged not to 'ritual' but to 'politics', to cultural relationships freed from the spell of charismatic authority.

ANTI-FASCIST CULTURE

Caudwell, Marcuse and Benjamin, in their different and unequal critical interventions, struck at the ideal foundations of Kulturkritik. But they were exceptional, more or less weightless figures, not only because they were Marxists, but because these writings, appearing first in the later 1930s, were, as a matter of chronological fate if not conscious purpose, at odds with the now-dominant line in Communist policy. All three proposed intransigently leftist critiques of bourgeois culture in a period when the international Communist movement, responding to the Nazi victory in Germany, had turned rightwards to seek a reconciliation with the forces of liberalism.

Between 1932 and 1935, the first initiatives towards a united front against fascism evolved into the co-ordinated policy and practice of the Popular Front, a formula entailing the restraint of anti-capitalist impulses in the interests of a cross-class 'democratic' alliance. Intellectuals, ostentatiously identified as such, took a conspicuous part at every stage in this process (Julien Benda rallied to the Association of Revolutionary Writers and Artists in 1933, and a year later put his name to the launch manifesto of the Comité de Vigilance des Intellectuels Anti-fascistes (Lefranc 1965: 433).) By the middle 1930s, they had become essential to it.

The great bonding theme of Popular Frontism – the diplomatic code in which Communist and liberal intellectuals might reach working agreements – was 'culture' in its most familiar sense as the common spiritual inheritance of worker and bourgeois. Caudwell's cultural theory implied a wholesale polarization of class against class. Marcuse saw liberal and fascist culture as formal equivalents, 'inward' and universalist in one case, 'heroically outward' and nationalist in the other (Marcuse 1972: 124f). There is no document of culture, Benjamin would write, that is not 'at the same time a document of barbarism' (Benjamin [1940] 1970: 258). But the official wisdom of the Popular Front was that culture was the light and inspiration of the (democratic) struggle against (fascist) barbarism. The controlling register of Popular Front discourse – elaborated in an international array of periodicals, books, organizations and events – was that of humanism militant: literature, art, spiritual values were the great stake and a precious resource in the common struggle against fascist inhumanity. Cultural 'aura' too worked its magic, in a characteristically modern form that Benjamin did not foresee. The set-piece International Congresses for the Defence of Culture, mounted in Paris and Madrid, were gatherings of stars: Benda, André Gide, Thomas Mann, Heinrich Mann, Aldous Huxley and E.M. Forster, among many others (Leroy and Roche 1986: 16f; Lottman 1982).

Political discord was never quite banished from these venues, where leftist and liberal critics of Communist orthodoxy insisted on being heard, and the coloration of Popular Front cultural activity varied from one country to another, in part because of local political circumstances. But these variations had a rationale that was itself uniform and official. If the defence of 'culture' entailed a renewed appeal to the universally human, it also called for a positive revaluation of the nation. In its first, more strongly political formulation – that of the Bulgarian Communist leader Dimitrov – the call to recover national tradition bore a critical charge: the valued past was that of the people and their struggles

(Heinemann 1985: 157–86). But the national is never so easily redefined, and in the wider cultural diplomacy of the Popular Fronts it came to be represented as the site of mediation between the writer and the masses (or liberal cultural tradition and Communist politics), as the universal in everyday, local attire. In this way, the perceived necessities of a political emergency facilitated a regression in the terms of cultural understanding – in the English case, to a national popular variation on Kulturkritik, which would persist well beyond its formative political occasion, into the post-war period.

3

WELFARE?

In Britain, during and after the Second World War, the 'intellectuals' politics' of the 1920s and 1930s turned from protest to policy. The historical condition of this shift was the great new theme of 'welfare': welfare in economic and social matters first of all, but also in education, broadcasting and the arts – that whole institutional complex of practices that might, or might not, be protected or sponsored or desired or criticized as 'culture'.

Post-elementary state education was made available to all, and compulsory to the age of 15. Merit rather than money determined access to the upper echelon of the new tripartite state system, the grammar school. Higher education expanded rapidly in the early post-war years, although from a tiny demographic base. Radio, continuing as a public monopoly, expanded and diversified its programming, but again – like education – on strict hierarchical assumptions. Access to television viewing widened dramatically, though without prejudice to paternalist control of the repertoire. The licensing of commercial television in the middle 1950s caused widespread foreboding, but in fact the new service was subject to significant public-service constraints. A government-funded council was created, succeeding the wartime Council for the Encouragement of Music and the Arts, to support the arts and promote wider interest in them. And in the bookshops, the shelves turned orange and blue, the colours of Penguin Books, a privately-owned BBC of the printed word (Morpurgo 1979).

Of course, pure commerce, too, was active in every paper shop and cinema, but in the old and new centres of policy, a common formula had been set in place. A minority culture, received and continuing, would be diffused to an ever-widening audience. All the terms of this summary should be noted. The expansion was real, but there was no fundamental questioning of what counted as cultural value or of the proper forms of cultural participation. Self-confirming traditions would now be unveiled for a deserving population. Culture – 'the best that is known and thought in the world', 'sweetness and light', in Arnold's famous gloss – would now, literally, be 'broad-cast'.

The formula governing this emerging world of policy and practice was a Victorian bequest. In its mid-century applications, it was to a great extent the achievement of the two salient tendencies in liberal minority culture between the wars: the Bloomsbury circle and the group around F.R. Leavis and *Scrutiny*. It is usual to stress the contrasts between the two formations. Bloomsbury was an upper-middle-class bohemia, a congeries of families and friends whose unity and security in the face of commercial pressure and ancestral philistinism were sustained by private money. *Scrutiny* was proudly petty-bourgeois, hostile to all metropolitan ornament and hereditary presumption, the self-conscious vanguard of a 'critical minority' that sought nothing but – and nothing less than – the recognition due to unaided intelligence. However, these social–stylistic differences were variants of a shared liberal formula, which both formations helped to promote after the war. John Maynard Keynes was not only the pioneering theorist of the new macro-economic policy; he also founded the Arts Council. Bloomsbury's free-thinking modernism was hardly consonant with Lord Reith's cultural preferences, yet that 'civilized' manner eventually lightened his own puritan tone in the BBC, just as it also became standard in the formerly 'middlebrow' cultural and recreational pages of the polite press. *Scrutiny's* insistence on careers open to talent appeared to find some acknowledgement in the weakening of class privilege in education – where, at the same time, Leavisian accents were more and more widely heard. The emergent styles of cultural seriousness, in education and in the media, were essentially generalizations, named or not, from these inter-war models.

However, amid the signs of liberal hegemony, the liberal intelligentsia itself was not free of discontent. Intellectual life had become narrower and meaner since the war, according to one Bloomsbury survivor. The twenties and thirties had been bohemian and cosmopolitan; the fifties were provincial and earnest, their tone set by 'lower-middlebrows' who approached the arts in the spirit of sanitary engineers (Spender 1953: 66–8). Among a younger generation inspired by Leavis, there were those who would have smiled at this caricature of themselves, who affirmed that their kind of intellectual was now poised to take possession of the heritage (Bradbury 1956: 469–77). But others of them were disturbed by post-war Britain (or England, as they would more typically say). *Scrutiny* itself, which closed down in 1953, had recoiled from the approach of educational reform. Leavis himself could see only further deterioration, the nearing extinction of English minority culture.

ELIOT'S WHOLE WAY OF LIFE

The year 1948 marked T.S. Eliot's apotheosis as a great man of English letters, opening with his elevation to the Order of Merit and ending with the award of the Nobel Prize. It was, of course, as a poet that he received these honours. Yet for a decade and more his energies had been significantly deployed in a different kind of intellectual effort. *The Idea of a Christian Society* (1939)

signalled an intensification of his already-evident interest in social theorizing, and coincided with the beginning of a period of
collaborative inquiry, in the setting of the Council on the
Christian Faith and the Common Life and its intellectual network, the Moot, during which he undertook his most ambitious
venture in cultural criticism. This took shape in the course of
1942 and was aired first in an essay, 'Notes Towards a Definition
of Culture', serialized in the *New English Weekly* early the next
year, and then in seminars conducted with Philip Mairet, the
Weekly's editor (Eliot 1943). It reached definitive form in 1948,
appearing as a book under the title – pointed now by a change of
article – *Notes Towards the Definition of Culture*.

Eliot's text is pervaded by his Christian beliefs – he dismissed
as 'illusion' the idea 'that there [could] be culture without religion' (1962: 70) – but not too much should be made of this. His
decisive assertions, far from depending logically on Christian assumptions, might have been made with equal force by an unbe-
liever. *Notes* proposed three related theses. First, culture, properly
understood, was of three kinds: that of *individuals*, that of *groups*
or *classes*, and that of *the whole society*. The first depended on the
second, and that in turn on the last, which was thus 'fundamental' (1962: 21). These three kinds of culture, which were also 'levels', were the natural accompaniments of an increasingly
differentiated social organization. They were, of course, distinct
in substance, but, also, and decisively, in form. They differed in
their proportions of 'conscious aim', which individuals might
pursue with greater effect than groups, and these far more effectively than a whole society. Indeed – and this was Eliot's second
thesis – culture as 'a whole way of life' was to a significant degree
unconscious, and for that reason was not amenable to direction at
all (pp. 19, 20). As he had written a few years earlier in the
Christian Newsletter, 'culture might be described as that which
cannot be planned, except by God' (Kojecký 1971, 194–5). It
was to be seen, rather, as an organism, both in its delicate articu-

lation of interdependent functions and in its modalities of growth and change.

These were the bases from which Eliot forwarded his third thesis, in direct opposition to Karl Mannheim's espousal of democratic elites. Viewed in the light of this essentially corporatist theory of culture and society, democratic elitism was triply deficient. First, it replicated the commonplace confusion of cultural kinds, supposing that what was appropriate for an individual, or for a group, was therefore appropriate for the many. Further, it entailed an 'atomistic' reduction of the social order, seeing an aggregate of interchangeable individuals where in reality there was an evolved hierarchical unity of parts. Finally, and in consequence of these associated shortcomings, it failed to understand the requirements of cultural continuity.

A traditional elite, a cluster of gifted individuals formed in and around the propertied classes, sustained by them and assimilating new talent on established terms, made for a certain continuity, even in adverse modern conditions.[1] But a planned system of social and cultural leadership based on merit rather than blood or money, in so far as it fulfilled its own criteria of operation, would actively maximize incoherence and discontinuity. Mannheim had foreseen this difficulty, but judged it less dangerous than a recrudescence of the old prerogatives (Mannheim 1940: 88–92). Eliot disagreed. Cultural responsibility entailed abstinence from programmatic intervention, a Burkean 'piety towards the dead, however obscure, and a solicitude for the unborn, however remote' (Eliot 1962: 44). Class privilege, transmitted through the institution of the family, was an irreplaceable warrant of cultural well-being. To undermine the one was to imperil the other. 'If [the reader] finds it shocking that culture and equalitarianism should conflict, if it seems monstrous to him that anyone should have 'advantages of birth'[,] I do not ask him to change his faith, I merely ask him to stop paying lip-service to culture' (p. 16).

The strategic point of Eliot's titular term 'definition' was clear. The *Oxford English Dictionary* entry that served as his epigraph offered, for those who paused to read it, an epitome of his cultural politics:

DEFINITION: 1. The setting of bounds; limitation (rare) – 1483

If he insisted on culture as a whole way of life, it was not in the interests of conceptual advance, and not to revalue the meanings of popular life. His purpose was precisely to 'limit' and 'set bounds' to post-war cultural diffusionism, to discredit the ambitions of educational liberalism as misguided and otiose. 'On the whole', he wrote, 'it would appear to be for the best that the great majority of human beings should go on living in the place in which they were born' (p. 52). The strategy of *Notes* as a whole was to enforce the same mock-solicitous logic in the space of cultural relations: it was for the best that the great majority should not aspire, or be taught to aspire, to anything more than their familiar lot.

Scrutiny commentators were unhappily aware that Eliot's insistence on the unconscious character of culture ran contrary to Arnold's activist educational vision (Bantock 1949; Cormican 1950; Pocock 1950). But Eliot had perceived what *Scrutiny*'s self-styled 'outlaws' could not: that the general sense of post-war policy was itself Arnoldian. Resisting the policy, he also sought to discredit the principle that glossed it. The Arnoldian tradition held that culture might tame anarchy, if only society's 'best selves' were granted their due authority and discretion. Eliot saw in this prospectus the anarchic subversion of intellectual society, the unwitting self-dissolution of received minority values and privileges. As a strategy, be it meliorist or defensive, cultural liberalism was, like democratic elitism, a contradiction in terms.

HOGGART AND THE ABUSES OF LITERACY

In the middle 1940s, when *Notes Towards the Definition of Culture* was written, Eliot's sense of English popular culture was already deeply anachronistic. His montage of the English everyday was, so to speak, a reprise of his own earliest impressions, one American newcomer's version of pastoral:

> [Culture in the widest of his three senses] includes all the characteristic activities and interests of a people: Derby Day, Henley Regatta, Cowes, the twelfth of August, a cup final, the dog races, the pin table, the dart board, Wensleydale cheese, boiled cabbage cut into sections, beetroot in vinegar, nineteenth-century Gothic churches and the music of Elgar.
>
> (Eliot 1962: 31)

At the turn of the 1960s, when he reissued the book without alteration, this vision of a world without cinema, broadcasting or print must have seemed a hallucination. Between the first and second editions of *Notes* , the cultural universe of the social majority had been extensively reordered, in part by those ominous education reforms and an associated widening of cultural opportunity, and in greater part through the ever more vigorous commercial traffic in words and images. 'Classless' was the widely promoted description of a process in which the inherited signs of English social caste were reworked as commodities, turned into styles and spectacles to enliven the mock-democratic world of mass commerce. Converging with marketing strategies in this, public policy sponsored a vision of classlessness – through equality of opportunity – but, precisely in doing so, instated the working class as a real cultural presence and topic. Among the effects of these co-operating tendencies was the emergence of a new minority in British intellectual life, a scattering of writers and artists of working-class origin, who now moved into the approved spaces of artistic and intellectual production, there to assert or explore the values and prospects of the half-known, half-acknowledged social world from which they had come and to which, more often than not, they remained committed.

One of these was Richard Hoggart. Born into the Leeds working class at the end of the First World War, Hoggart made his way through a local grammar school and thence to the university, graduating in English Literature on the eve of the Second. After wartime service, he joined the Department of Adult Education at Hull University, from which he worked as a tutor until the end of the fifties. Hoggart's first book was a conventional work of literary criticism: *W.H. Auden*. However, he was also writing short sketches of working-class life for the Labour left weekly *Tribune*, where T.R. Fyvel had succeeded George Orwell as literary editor. And by the beginning of the 1950s, he was clarifying the terms of another kind of project, 'a new and natural extension', as he later described it, of 'the true stream of English studies' into the landscape of contemporary culture (Hoggart 1992: 10).

His critical point of reference was Q.D. Leavis's *Fiction and the Reading Public* (1932), the founding text of *Scrutiny*'s cultural diagnostics. Twenty years on, Hoggart proposed 'a sort of guide or textbook to aspects of popular culture' that would make good the unfulfilled promise of Leavis's title by integrating the critical study of texts within an analysis of the already-formed culture of their readers: 'one had to know very much more about how people used much of the stuff which to us might seem merely dismissible trash, before one could speak confidently about the effects it might have' (Hoggart 1990: 134–5). The work, whose precise focus would be on the impact of mass-marketed cultural forms on the inherited ethos of the working class, was to be called *The Abuses of Literacy*.

The book eventually published in 1957 differed significantly from its early design. The title was shorn of its provocative first syllable, in an attempt to mollify a publisher fearful of crushing litigation, and for the same reason, Hoggart was obliged to pastiche much of his printed evidence rather than quote it. But the major change was structural. The original analytic scheme furnished only half of *The Uses of Literacy*, its second part. This was now preceded by a long, hybrid discourse – part autobiography and memoir, part exemplary fiction, part social documentary – on working-class life between the wars, offered as the necessary context for the analysis of popular culture in the fifties.

It was this reflection on 'an "older" order' that gave the book its tone, distinguishing it very clearly from its Leavisian antecedent and also from a left-wing inspiration like Orwell. Hoggart wrote here with the assurance and feeling of one who had come from the world he described, with an unflagging consciousness of Britain's class order and his own dislocated relation to it. He was, in his own later words, 'a once-born socialist' immovably committed to the welfare of his native class (Hoggart 1990: 78). The contemporary cultural materials that he went on to dissect – the glossy magazines, the pulp fiction, the popular song lyrics – did not express the traditional ethos of this class and did not (yet) define it, he argued. The populism of the cultural market was an 'approach' from the outside, exploiting inherited strengths and weaknesses alike, threatening to reduce its working-class audience to a demoralized lower caste. It was a kind of spiritual 'robbery'.

However, altered social sensibility and political alignment did not undermine discursive continuity. Hoggart's evaluative idiom was saturated with *Scrutiny*'s clinical metaphorics of health and sickness, vigour and debility. His writing was at times quite possessed by the spirit of the Leavises: 'The hedonistic but passive barbarian who rides in a fifty-horse-power bus for threepence, to see a five-million-dollar film for one-and-eightpence, is not simply a social oddity; he is a portent' (Hoggart 1958: 250). His closing remarks read like an oath of allegiance: here was one individual's 'contribution to a much wider discussion, a single diagnosis offered for scrutiny' (p. 344).

Hoggart professedly saw *The Uses of Literacy* as disjunct, and has remained unmoved by those who have read it as a single composition (1992: 5). But it is just here, in the forms of the book seen as a whole, that his discursive affiliation is more strongly registered. The dominant mode of the work is narrative; the story it tells is of decline already far gone and perhaps unarrestable. The contrast that emerges in his account is not simply between two periods in the life of working-class Leeds. His story begins with an evocation of his country-born grandmother, with her customary knowledges and skills, then remembers two generations of native city-dwellers, and turns finally to observe the life-patterns of a fourth generation, the working-class young of the early 1950s. Hoggart was aware of the temptation to nostalgia, and tried repeatedly to check it. But his qualifications were too punctually stated, too evidently concessionary in their acknowledgement of an improved material existence, to remake what was a canonical narrative of the descent from rural tradition into urban-industrial anomie.

The two-part organization of the text recalls Orwell's *The Road to Wigan Pier*, and its rhetorical strategy is of the same kind, though potentially more effective. In both cases, a record of experience purports to validate a critical analysis: because I have known this life, the tacit reasoning goes, I may reliably make this judgement. Yet the truth must be otherwise. Memory is a construction of the past, and in Hoggart's descriptions (as in Orwell's) there was much that was already familiar from literary convention. In practice, Hoggart's writing appealed to a quite different kind of moral authority, as was evident in its strategy of quotation. The text draws heavily on working-class idiom, and on the actual or mimicked words of commercial culture. These are clearly marked, by punctuation or typography, as evidence for analysis; they might be termed *object*-quotations. At the same time, the text avails itself of another kind of citation, which is granted a different status. These are the epigraphs that introduce his own words, and the many phrases that occur with little or no formal marking, woven into the syntax of his own discourse as elements of itself. They are, in contrast, *subject*-quotations. Amplifying Hoggart's own prose voice, Locke, Tocqueville, Arnold, Gorky, Benda, Auden, Forster, Lawrence, Yeats and others form an entire chorus of wisdom and insight. Theirs is the true authority of the book, which he upholds against the cynical libertarianism of mass commerce: the collective voice of *culture* raised against a wayward *civilization*.

This conceptual binary governed the vision of *The Uses of Literacy* and accounted for its most significant absence: the record of working-class self-organization in politics, work and education. Hoggart's disarming explanation for the omission was that these were the interests of a small, 'earnest' minority untypical of their class. A stronger, though not more sympathetic explanation would cite the spontaneous perceptual effect of the convention that framed his analysis: that of Kulturkritik. The binary culture/civilization classifies all social tissue as either quality or quantity, purpose or mechanism, end or means, and the logical effect of this construction is to render politics unintelligible as a meaningful social activity: rarefied as 'values' or banalized as practical administration, its specific reality as a form of social practice is lost. Working-class political activists are no smaller a minority than the far less class-typical bourgeois novelist. If the one seemed so obviously less meaningful than the other, it was because in Hoggart's received scheme of analysis, politics as such was a secondary moral reality.

'Labour Leavisism' would be one summary of Hoggart's distinctively bifocal cultural vision. Yet he was both less demonstrative and less desperate than these categories suggest. A moment's reflection on his subsequent work prompts a more exact characterization. Throughout his career – in the Arts Council and UNESCO as well as in public education – Hoggart thought to serve his class of origin and at the same time to serve culture through the 'practical criticism' of policy and administration. His model institutions, the three volumes of his memoirs confirm, were adult education, the BBC and Penguin Books. Hoggart's specific novelty was to renew, in modified social conditions, the tradition of Kulturkritik and the liberal mission of the public-service intellectual. In him, the post-war British Labour movement found its own Matthew Arnold.

4

A RECKONING

Between the writing of Hoggart's *The Uses of Literacy* and its publication came 1956, a year of shocks and portents that confounded the settled imagination of British politics and culture and unveiled the shapes of domestic and international relations after the post-war reconstruction. The Anglo-French expedition to seize the Suez canal, which had been nationalized by Egypt's revolutionary government, ended in military and diplomatic humiliation. The episode dramatized the predicament of an imperial ruling caste that could neither check its hereditary arrogance in the face of anti-colonial revolution nor readily accept its subaltern standing in an international capitalist order now dominated by the USA. Popular revulsion from the Suez adventure was one sign that, at home as much as abroad, old political maxims were losing their potency. And the scandalous cultural successes of the year – Colin Wilson's *The Outsider*, John Osborne's *Look Back in Anger* and the film *Rock Around the Clock* – gave early warning of new collective sensibilities in the making: eclectic, undeferential, impatient, and always and ever 'young'. This was also a moment of crisis for the left. Josef Stalin had died three years earlier. The year opened with Nikita Khrushchev's post-mortem denunciation of his predecessor's lawless, bloodstained rule over the Soviet Union – and ended, in bloody irony, with the crushing of the popular revolt in Hungary by Red Army tanks. The effect of these revelations in word and deed was convulsive, throughout the Communist movement. The British party lost one-fifth of its members, as some 7,000 militants, including a disproportionate number of intellectuals, resigned or were driven out. Such were the formative conditions of 'the New Left' and of a new phase in the history of discourse on culture.

Two journals, both founded in 1957, formed the intellectual nuclei of the New Left. *The New Reasoner* was edited from the North of England by two ex-Communist historians, John Saville and Edward Thompson. Having begun as an irregular oppositional organ within the party in direct response to Khrushchev's revelations, the journal was dedicated to the moral renewal of Communism under the banner of a 'socialist humanism'. Ex-Communists also featured among the editors and collaborators of *Universities and Left Review* (ULR), and the theme of a post-Stalinist socialist humanism was reiterated there. However, the more emphatic concern of the journal, which emerged from a group of Oxford students, was to elaborate an analysis and a programme that would supersede not only orthodox Communism but Labourism as well, a thoroughgoing socialist critique of contemporary, welfare-capitalist Britain.[1] A *new* left for a new historical *situation*: this was ULR's distinctive appreciation of the intellectual challenge facing socialists after 1956. 'The New Conservatism' and Britain's modified class relations in a period of expanding social provision and imperial decline were the subject of Stuart Hall's opening contribution to the review's agenda. This was followed, in the second issue, by a symposium on working-class culture occasioned by the newly published *Uses of Literacy*.

It is worth noting, nearly fifty years later, just how critically Hoggart's classic was received in the New Left's leading forum. The editors' opening question was courteous but incisive: 'Would a direct account in terms of readership reaction differ from Hoggart's content-analysis of the publications themselves?'[2]

John McLeish likened the book's protagonist to 'a visiting anthropologist of a behaviourist persuasion' (1957: 32). Gwyn Illtyd Lewis (1957) matched Hoggart's cultural apprehensions with his own fears of 'commercial devitalization' in the English-speaking population of Wales. The cumulative implication of these comments was grave. Hoggart had not so much studied readers' use of mass print culture as inferred their subjective disposition from its contents; his relation to them, far from empathetic, was that of a clinician observing patterns of stimulus and response – and the controlling theme of his analysis, as Lewis glossed it, was surely familiar. In other words, *The Uses of Literacy* in practice reanimated the critical discourse it offered to supersede, inflecting but not displacing the conventions of Leavisian Kulturkritik. Raymond Williams, in the opening contribution to the symposium, saluted Hoggart's 'deep loyalty to his own people', but then, the more tellingly for that, made two fundamental objections. In present conditions, he insisted, 'working-class materialism' must be defended as a 'humane' value. And Hoggart was mistaken in excluding working-class activism as a 'minority' case, in effect relegating the culture of specialized class representatives to the status of social eccentricity. This minority, as he would later maintain in a recorded conversation with Hoggart, inherited and sustained a general history of struggle for democracy, trade unions and socialism – 'the high working-class tradition' (Williams 1957: 31–2; Williams and Hoggart 1960: 26–30). The implication of these remarks was fundamental. In reclaiming material desire as a moral good and politics as a *'high* tradition', Williams was not simply adjusting the balance of Hoggart's analysis, he was disorganizing its basic terms, and so intimating the possibility of an alternative way of seeing, beyond the perceptual scheme of Kulturkritik.

RAYMOND WILLIAMS: BEYOND CULTURE-AND-SOCIETY

Williams resembled Hoggart in his origins and career trajectory. A few years younger, Williams too had been born into a working-class family, risen through a local grammar school to study English at university, served in the army during the war, then gone to work in adult education, where he combined his ordinary duties with various independent writing and publishing projects. However, the differences of formation were at least as significant. Williams's family was actively socialist. Whereas Hoggart came from an urban English working class, Williams's early years were spent in the mixed-class environment of a Welsh village. Hoggart completed his formal education in his home town, where his left-wing convictions developed without assuming definite programmatic form. Williams, in contrast, crossed the national and social border to Cambridge, where, as he later recalled, the Communist Party and the University Socialist Club provided the staples of his intellectual life (Williams 1979). These variations on an apparently common biographical scheme formed two quite different politico-cultural sensibilities: in the one case, a congenital class tenderness sustaining allegiance to the dominant traditions of British labourism; in the other, a more radical and more consequential political training combined with an egalitarian self-possession conceding nothing to the deep fatalism of England's culture of class.

Formed once in the confident Communist sub-culture of the late 1930s, Williams underwent a difficult, protracted re-formation in the altered conditions he found upon returning to complete his studies in 1945. Although still a Communist, he was now outside the party, distrustful of its official publicity and unimpressed by its cultural orientation (Williams 1979: 61–77; 1980: 240–1). The red network of his first Cambridge period had collapsed, and the student socialists with whom he now sought constructive engagement took their cultural bearings from Leavis. The immediate outcome of these new associations was the short-lived journal *Politics and Letters*, which, together with its sibling, *The Critic*, explored an alliance of independent socialist politics with literary-cultural themes familiar from *Scrutiny*. This initiative has been mourned as the lost British counterpart of Sartre's *Les Temps Modernes*, but it is difficult to imagine that unrealized future (Barnett, 1976). *Politics and Letters* – the broken register of the title was sign enough – was the expression of a certain intellectual crisis, not a coherent intervention in it, and would have ended in confusion had not circumstantial difficulties foreclosed its development. The ground of this crisis, as Williams began to understand it, was the meaning of 'culture' itself, and 'a long line of thinking about culture' that had been 'appropriat[ed] ... to what were by now decisively reactionary positions' (1979: 97).

Out of this perception, which had begun to form as a response to the Cambridge Leavisians and then been clarified with the appearance of Eliot's *Notes*, came the inquiry that led, over the next eight years, to *Culture and Society*.[3] If the primary motive of the book was political, its critical strategy was, crucially, historical. The idea of culture, as a privileged term of evaluation, had emerged during the Industrial Revolution, Williams argued, and must then be understood as a critical actor in the remaking of social meanings that attended it. In order to undo the moral spell of 'culture', it would be necessary to retrace the process of its formation. 'For what I see in the history of this word, in its structure of meanings, is a wide and general movement in thought and feeling. ... I wish to show the emergence of *culture* as an abstraction and an absolute' (Williams [1958] 1961: 17) – as a separate and higher social sphere, from which final moral judgement might be given and something of a moral alternative sustained.

Organized as a long sequence of author-specific analyses, *Culture and Society* was in substance the history of a discourse, its formation, variation and transmutation. Williams analysed the progressive rarefaction of *culture* over the 150-year span from Edmund Burke, the great scourge of the French Revolution, to F.R. Leavis. He showed how a cause that had taken shape as the defence of a whole and present social order then narrowed, in stages, to the lament for an irrecoverable past; how, as its actual social bases weakened, its claims mounted towards the absolute; how, by the middle of the twentieth century it had been reduced to the desperate self-assertion of a specialized minority – *Scrutiny* – as the only sure trustees of an unattainable general spiritual welfare. Williams identified fundamental breaks where there was the strongest evidence of continuity, for example, acknowledging Williams Morris's romantic medievalism, but also insisting on the significance of his communism. He identified continuity where there was the most confident proclamation of a new departure – seeing in the Marxism of the thirties not only Communism but a persisting belief in romantic visions of art. Then, in a long concluding chapter, he explored the meaning of this complex, unfinished history, and situated himself within it:

> The idea of culture is a general reaction to a general and major change in the condition of our common life. Its basic element is its effort at total qualitative assessment. ... General change, when it has worked itself clear, drives us back on our general designs, which we have to learn to look at again, and as a whole.
>
> (Williams [1958] 1961: 285)

The meanings of 'culture' were not unequivocal: 'The word ... cannot automatically be pressed into service as any kind of social directive. ... The arguments which can be grouped under its heading do not point to any inevitable action or affiliation' (p. 285). Yet they 'define ... a common field' and subserve, apparently, a common purpose: 'The working-out of the idea of culture is a slow reach again for control' (p. 285).

Formulations like this, abstract in reference and seemingly inclusive in address, were themselves less than unequivocal. *Culture
and Society* was evidently a statement from the left, yet it was unclear what specific intellectual and political orientations it sponsored. The most influential interpretation, at first offered
affirmatively and, since the early 1970s, more often stated as a
charge, was that the book proposed a moral refoundation of socialism in the tradition of English cultural humanism, that it
was, in a phrase that became routine, a 'left-Leavisite' alternative
to the intellectual ruin of Stalinism.[4] A less-well-known interpretation agreed that Williams's deep theme was the necessary and
desirable continuation of that tradition in the contemporary left,
but argued that his intervention was for just that reason *communist* in character. In fact, it paralleled, in its own idiom, the post-
war orientation of Party cultural analysis, which sought to trace a
'national' lineage for Marxist thought, in keeping with the
Popular Front traditions of the 1930s and the post-war political
strategy of a 'British road to socialism' (1979: 112). There is, in
the end, little difference between these readings, and both find
support in textual and contextual evidence. The substantive concepts of Williams's title, *Culture* and *Society*, were those of the tradition he discussed, but they seemed often to exert reflexive
control over his own discourse, deflecting his analytic and evaluative priorities away from political reason proper towards a
'higher', finally 'common' moral ground – the familiar orientation
of Kulturkritik. It is striking, too, that Williams conceived his
revaluation of English Kulturkritik in the same years that saw
the Communist Party devote itself to recovering Coleridge, the
Romantics, Carlyle, Ruskin and Morris as authentically national
resources for the left. The historian Edward Thompson was
prominent in this politico-cultural initiative, and kindred themes
were sounded in *Politics and Letters* by another Communist scholar,
Christopher Hill.[5]

However, neither line of interpretation leads to a secure historical estimate of *Culture and Society*. The Communist Party's cultural initiative was predominantly nationalist in thrust, an ill-judged attempt to resist the emerging North Atlantic culture of the Cold War by marshalling an essentially 'progressive' English tradition against the 'decadence' and 'barbarism' of New York and Hollywood. The result, as evidenced in the Party's cultural quarterly, *Arena*, was a crude national populism, often mawkish or phobic, tendentious where not self-deluding or simply dishonest. There was nothing of this in *Culture and Society*, nor anything of *Arena*'s ready identification with the British Marxism of the 1930s – from which, indeed, Williams took a clear, cool distance ([1958] 1961: 258–75). *Arena*'s repertoire included a serviceable pastiche of the *Scrutiny* manner, defining the 'function of a literary magazine', its 'lonely' function, as 'the maintenance ... of fundamental critical standards', the pursuit of 'critical vitality' as a condition of 'creative vitality'.[6] In such moments, as in its wholesale condemnation of (American) mass-cultural production, *Arena*'s greater affinity was with Hoggart's *The Uses of Literacy*. There, of course, the use of that register signified a real discursive continuity from Leavis. In Williams, the marks of continuity were not even, properly speaking, residual. They were rather the scars of a specific, unfinished engagement in alien country. It seems preferable, with all qualifications entered, to view *Culture and Society* as Williams himself saw it, as 'an oppositional work – not primarily designed to found a new position' but to undermine an existing one (Williams 1979: 98).[7]

Three considerations support this self-description – and in fact enhance its claim. Williams's attempt 'to counter the appropriation' of cultural criticism for reactionary purposes was not, as continuist interpretations must assume, the prelude to a socialist *re*appropriation of it. On the contrary, his historical summary of the tradition, although generous, was fundamentally critical, speaking of the idea of culture as 'an abstraction and an absolute'. Neither did he suggest that culture in this sense might be democratized by expansion, privilege redeeming itself in the gesture of welfare. On the contrary, he expressly rejected high-cultural diffusionism, and characterized the liberal intellectual tradition of 'service' as an adapted form of bourgeois individualism that sought only to limit the damage of a social order whose basic principle it took for granted ([1958] 1961: 312). Against both forms of the dominant ideology, he set the alternative principle of 'solidarity' – and this not as an ethical abstraction and absolute, but as the historical achievement of capitalism's distinctive form of labour, the working class (p. 313). With this plain endorsement of working-class creativity, Williams affirmed the possibility that positive cultural values could be shaped in and by, as well as against, the social relations of modern 'civilization'. In doing so, he marked a position beyond the imaginative range of culture-and-society.

FROM PATERNALISM TO DEMOCRACY

Appearing in 1958, *Culture and Society* announced the possibility of 'a new general theory of culture' and looked forward to 'a full restatement of principles, taking the theory of culture as a theory of relations between elements in a whole way of life' ([1958] 1961: 11–12). By then, Williams had already begun writing *Essays and Principles*, the book eventually published three years later as *The Long Revolution*. 'We live in an expanding culture,' Williams had written, 'yet we spend much of our energy regretting the fact, rather than seeking to understand its nature and conditions' (1961: 12). *The Long Revolution* was, for the greater part, a sustained theoretical and historical effort towards that understanding, and, throughout, was governed by the ambition to clarify a politics adequate to that 'expanding culture'. *Culture and Society* had attacked the prevailing critical conception of the epoch as that of 'the masses ... low in taste and habit'; in a short, prospective essay also published in 1958, Williams proposed his counter-thesis: 'culture is ordinary'.

Implicit in this disarmingly ordinary adjective were a theoretical proposition, a corresponding social revaluation and the germ of a cultural politics, all three brought into focus in a long opening shot:

> The bus stop was outside the cathedral. I had been looking at the Mappa Mundi, with its rivers out of Paradise, and at the chained library, where a party of clergymen had got in easily, but where I had waited an hour and cajoled a verger before I even saw the chain. Now, across the street, a cinema advertised the *Six-Five Special* and a cartoon version of *Gulliver's Travels*. The bus arrived, with a driver and a conductress deeply absorbed in each other. We went out of the city, over the old bridge, and on through the orchards and the green meadows and the fields red under the plough. Ahead were the Black Mountains, and we climbed among them, watching the steep fields end at the grey walls, beyond which the bracken and heather and whin had not yet been driven back. To the east, along the ridge, stood the line of grey Norman castles; to the west, the fortress wall of the mountains. Then, as we still climbed, the rock changed under us. Here, now, was limestone, and the line of the early iron workings along the scarp. The farming valleys, with their scattered white houses, fell away behind. Ahead of us were the narrower valleys: the steel-rolling mill, the gasworks, the grey terraces, the pitheads. The bus stopped, and the driver and conductress got out, still absorbed. They had done this journey so often, and seen all its stages.
>
> (Williams 1989: 3)

Much in this landscape is familiar from Eliot or Leavis or Hoggart. But the framing and sequence of the narrative offered an alternative to their ways of seeing. The familiar, fatal oppositions between elite and popular, culture and commerce, town and country, past and present, continuity and change, sensibility and machinery,

Arnold's 'best' and 'ordinary selves' – the entire conceptual repertoire of 'culture and society' – were disordered in this complex
time–space of social meaning, the shared element of everyday existence.

Culture, as Williams now proposed to theorize it, was the
mode in which all human existence defined and evaluated itself.
Strictly speaking, the very phrase 'culture *and* society' was a confusion. The two basic processes of culture were learning and discovery, the relay of established meanings and the probing of new
ones, and neither, in a period of significant expansion, was adequately served by the prevailing dual order of commerce plus
public service. The case against the capitalist market in culture
was familiar (most recently, in Hoggart's version), and, although
intensified in Williams's theoretical perspective, was not altered
by it. The inbuilt logic of market activity was philistine, inter-
ested in any kind of expansion that might show a profit, but indifferent or hostile to all else. Yet the alternative of public
provision – 'common payment, for common services' – was hob-
bled not only by the usual complaint of ruinous expense but by
the locked imagination of minority culture, to which Williams
now posed a twofold challenge. It was a commonplace belief of
liberal and conservative cultural criticism that the educational
reforms of the later nineteenth century had engendered the trivi-
alizing mass journalism of the twentieth, and it was a commonplace of argument that, with money as with culture, the bad
tended to drive out the good. Both propositions were demonstrably
false, Williams retorted, and inadmissible as valid objections to
enhanced educational provision. However, this counter-insistence
was not offered as reassurance, for it was implicit in his theoretical concept of culture that 'growth' entailed something other
than simple 'extension':

> We should not seek to extend a ready-made culture to the be-
> nighted masses. We should accept, frankly, that if we extend

our culture, we shall change it: some that is offered will be radically criticized. ... I would not expect the working people of
England to support works which, after proper and patient
preparation, they could not accept. ... [If] we understand cultural growth, we shall know that it is a continued offering for
common acceptance, that we should not, therefore, try to determine in advance what should be offered, but clear the chan-
nels and let all the offerings be made, taking care to give the
difficult full space, the original full time, so that it is a real
growth, and not just a wider confirmation of old rules.

(Williams 1989: 16)

Fellow socialists found much to question in a passage like this,
then and in later years. 'Common', if offered as a description of
existing cultural relations, appeared to deny the actual inequalities and antagonisms of capitalism as 'a whole way of life'
(Thompson 1961). And, if offered as the keyword of a critical anthropology (for, as Williams believed, any culture must be in
some sense common, in order to be a culture at all), it appeared to
float into empty ethical space – as 'an abstraction and an absolute'. The recourse to the first-person plural strengthened suspi-
cions on these grounds, as also, in a strategic sense, did the irenic
language of 'offering' and 'growth'. It is true – whatever else may
or may not be true – that Williams's writing at this time inclined
too much to emollience. But it is also true, and of greater historical importance then and now, that some of the best criticism of
these ambiguities coexisted with them, in the same pages. There
was much still to rethink and to discover, but by the turn of the
1960s Williams had established the irreducible distance between
Kulturkritik in all its variants – reactionary or reforming – and
an integrally socialist politics of culture. 'Paternalism', the high-
minded format of cultural growth in welfare Britain, was not
only inadequate as a counter to its far more vigorous 'commercial'
other; it was itself mystified, and politically objectionable as a

modified version of 'authoritarian cultural organization'. The true alternative, Williams maintained, in his 1961 lecture 'Communications and Community', lay in *democratic* and *pluralist* participation in the institutions and practices of culture, a 'common' evaluation-in-process of an undecided future (1989: 23–31). Look again at the bus crew in that small allegory of culture. It is their labour that makes the narrative possible: the connections they sustain are a basic condition of what the observing passenger can see and report. But about them, and especially about their relation to the cultural complex they move through, the reader can know virtually nothing, because the Williams-figure, so knowledgeable and attentive, declines to interpret them. Paternalism always knows in advance what 'the masses' really need. Commerce always knows in advance what paternalism fears, that what the customers actually want is something else. In the enigmatic figure of the bus crew, Williams indicates an alternative principle (and it is here a principle, not an affectation of personal ignorance): no one may claim to know what 'the masses' are or want until they speak.[8]

PART II

CULTURAL STUDIES

1

A THEORY

Kulturkritik spoke in the name of a rarefied cluster of human values (culture) that survived in and against the prevailing generality of discourse (civilization). This distinction might be grounded in the nature of being, as with Julien Benda, but more commonly it was historical. The crucial term of historical definition, the social substance of tradition, might be a nation or a class, or a condensation of both, but in any case, culture was the true whole or universal, to be asserted against the false generality of modernity, with its riot of particular social interests. If culture was hardly the realm of freedom (a shallow, suspect value for this discursive tradition), nevertheless it incarnated the human potential for moral discretion and responsibility, for disciplined exploration, in radical contrast with civilization, the realm of pragmatic necessity, in which the inertial forces of passion and interest, Mann's 'classes and masses', dominated all else. Culture so understood was by necessary definition a practice of agonistic evaluation: any adequate appreciation of its inherited meanings entailed the most rigorous dealing with the spontaneous counter-suggestions of civilization. It was not permissible to relax in the name of a generous or sanguine pluralism: that was the logic of capitulation. Nor was there virtue in a habit of contemplative refusal: culture was the threatened mode of existence of valid – because truly general – social authority, which must be reaffirmed if not in some way restored to potency. Metacultural discourse bore within itself the intimation of good governance of the wayward whole.

The formation of a new discourse on culture – and, from the 1970s, the emergent institution of cultural studies – entailed a threefold challenge to this tradition. First, there would be *a radical expansion of the corpus*, the field of relevant inquiry, to include everyday modernity: any variety of the making of meaning, the whole social world of sense, might now be opened to examination. In itself, of course, this was no novelty. Anything but dismissive of what some thought to explore as 'popular culture', the antecedent tradition was obsessed with it. The Leavises and *Scrutiny* had dealt extensively with the practices and institutions of mass civilization. Also, Hoggart's *Uses of Literacy* showed that Kulturkritik could accommodate just such a radically expanded corpus, together with significant displacements of social sensibility and commitment, without conceptual strain. The second, more important condition of a new departure was the *unification* and *procedural equalization* of the field of inquiry. Even in its more historicist and sociological varieties, Kulturkritik was drawn to essentialist distinctions between culture, in the reserved, positive sense, and the other world of everyday (un)meaning, civilization. It was narcissistic in critical character, moving in a closed circle of value: the objects it contemplated, where they did not conform to its own self-image, were not recognizable at all. From now on, in contrast, it would be necessary to unify all signifying forms and practices in a single category – culture as the instance of meaning in society – and to insist, as a matter of procedure, that received conceptions of literary and artistic value should not predetermine the scope and purpose of inquiry. This second challenge resolved the ambiguity of the first, without yet securing the terms of the new departure. Had it been only an inclusive and procedurally uniform inquiry into the social world of sense, the emerging cultural studies would have been a variety of the existing discipline of anthropology, a research programme devoted to the 'superorganic' or 'symboling' life of human groups – though now in industrial rather than older and marginal societies (White 1975). It is, indeed, a real variety, but not the one that has been decisive. The defining aim of what would become Cultural Studies proper was to demystify the presumptive *authority* of Kulturkritik and the formations so defended, to undermine it and indeed supersede it. The motivation, all along, has been political.

WILLIAMS: CREATION IS ORDINARY

The formative conditions of this new discourse, we have already seen, were themselves political. The crises of the Communist and Labour traditions, in a period of significant economic and cultural change, gave it lasting definition. There was a further condition to be met, however, or, as it were, an objective logical proviso. The received idea of cultural authority was not merely a naturalized version of specific social and institutional affiliations, and would survive a challenge that pressed only so far against it. After all, Eliot and Leavis had in effect opposed each other in such terms, but on the shared ground of minority culture. The new discourse could secure its intellectual position only by digging out the foundations of the old one, the philosophical commonplaces that underpinned it. There would have to be a fresh initiative in general theory. This was the first and the crucial aim of *The Long Revolution*.

'Culture is ordinary', Williams had said. However, he now continued, there are, essentially, no 'ordinary' activities, if by 'ordinary' we mean the absence of creative interpretation and effort ([1961] 1965: 54). With this, he suspended the ages-old premiss of Western thinking about art. Surveying the record of aesthetic formulation in the English tradition, Williams underlined the persistent dualism of 'art' and 'reality' (p. 35). This divorce could be understood in opposite ways. Art might be parasitic, as Plato had claimed, a mere fiction twice removed from the fundamental reality of the Forms, which were the object of philosophy. Or, as in the contrasting estimate of the Aristotelian doctrine, it might be a mode of knowledge in its own right, giving access to the most general truths. But in either case, the basic dualism held good: on the one hand, a primary reality, and, on the other, the work of representing it. The Renaissance tradition confirmed and embellished the notion of art as special revelation, as a kind of creation, opposing it again to 'reality', but also, sometimes – and this was crucial – to a lesser, non-inspired kind of apprehension of that reality. By the turn of the nineteenth century, this old dualism had attained its definitive modern intensity. In Romantic thought, the superior cognitive powers of art became associated with a specific mental faculty, the imagination, and with a special kind of individual, the artist. Williams saw positive development in this record of thinking from Antiquity to Romanticism. It showed the strengthening assertion of specifically human powers against the persisting claims of religious tradition. Yet, as he also noted, this long transition from a religious to a secular–humanist identity was ambiguous, and could also involve the reinvention of old priestly norms in a modern guise. The terms of the ancient dualism between art and reality were not only ontological, they were also psychological and, implicitly, even social. 'Art', understood as the exercise of the creative imagination by the few whom it fully endowed, was henceforward set against a 'reality' that included not only a given world of objects but also a commonplace subjectivity that merely registered its phenomena – not only things but our 'ordinary' perception of them.

In fact, Williams went on to claim, the purported dualism of art and reality was 'false', and should now be displaced by a new, scientifically grounded theory of creativity. In the received understanding, creativity involved 'exceptional' rather than 'natural seeing'. It was a rare supplement to the generic human norm. However, contemporary research in the biology of perception had invalidated all such distinctions, showing that all seeing is conventional. 'Each one of us *has to learn to see*' (p. 33). There exists, in respect of any perceiving subject, an independent reality, including objects and other subjects, but it is never simply given as an intelligible world. 'Reality *as we experience it* is ... a human creation', and 'all our experience', notwithstanding our intuitions of its immediacy, 'is a human version of the world we inhabit' (p. 34). To come to see, then, to enter into 'experience', entails acquiring a set of 'rules', of which individuals are 'bearers'. Such rules are historical, variable through the changing times and spaces of the human environment, and must therefore undergo more or less radical revisions, each involving new learning. They are also, inevitably, collective: 'we learn to see a thing by learning to describe it', and, thus, since the means and schemes of description, adequate or not, are always already in place, by participating in a common world of meaning, the sphere of communication. Learning and communication, then, are the substantive processes of culture, which, moreover, is not simply an image of the world but one of its modes of constitution. Without these processes, it would be impossible to posit an intelligible world. They are in this basic sense fully 'creative' – and yet, it also follows, in no way 'exceptional'. Creation, on this account, is one of the banalities of social–historical 'nature'. Creation is ordinary.

Rethinking the anthropological and social significance of creativity in this way, Williams thought to work through the opposed versions of culture as special, superordinate value and culture as 'a whole way of life', and in this way to initiate a coherent and critical theory and politics of the domain of social meaning. The attempt was inevitably controversial – among conservatives and liberals, of course, but also on the left. The recurring matter for objection – it has, at this date, become a hereditary exercise in disputation – was Williams's emphasis on 'common' meanings, on 'community' and 'communication' (Thompson 1961; Eagleton 1976). The political implication of this elective vocabulary seemed to be a strategic gradualism, in which capitalist relations of property and power might be dissolved through a process of 'growth'. Philosophically, it appeared as evidence of an unsurmounted humanism traceable to the impact of F.R. Leavis. Questions of political strategy need not directly concern us here, though the matter of the political as a social form is central to my argument, and I will return to this later. There will also be more to say about the philosophical issue. For now, a few observations may serve to reduce these problems to something nearer their actual scale, and, at the same time, to place the emphasis where it belongs, on Williams's discursive break with Kulturkritik. The analytic sequence of *The Long Revolution* moves from abstract to concrete. Opening with an anthropological account of 'the creative mind', it goes on to discuss issues in the general theory of social relations, and introduces the specifically cultural concepts of 'social character' and 'structure of feeling' ('The Analysis of Culture'). There follows a critique of specifically bourgeois representations of individuality and social order, and then a suite of studies in English cultural history (education, literacy, the press, language, writers, dramatic forms, the contemporary novel). The book closes with a synoptic analysis of a contemporary situation ('Britain in the 1960s'). The analysis of culture as 'making common', or 'communication', sets out from a psycho-biological theory of species constants: that is to say, from an order of abstraction in which, as a principle of scientific procedure, socially specific forms and relations of commonality – of property and labour, for example – have no place. And if the rhetorical insistence of these terms seems greater than theoretical definition requires, it is because they are simultaneously involved in a struggle against modern literary common sense. The relevant contraries of 'common' and 'communication', clearly visible in the text, are not such categories as power, inequality, struggle and revolution. They are the special creative individual of Romantic tradition, and the self-enclosing projects of modernist aesthetics (as Archibald McLeish famously declared, 'A poem should not mean/But be') and the common-sense reduction of the 'creative' to the 'new' (Williams [1961] 1965: 46–51). The book as a whole is shaped by this purpose. As a work of history as well as theory and method, it is again structured by specific critical engagements, challenging the canonical Leavisian narrative of decline on its own favoured sites – education, language and the press – and naming and endorsing an alternative grand narrative of modernity as 'the long revolution'. There was even more of Kulturkritik here than was commonly suggested, and most of it was debris.

MARXISM AND CULTURAL THEORY

Williams's 'theory of culture as a theory of relations between elements in a whole way of life' was socialist in political affiliation, historical in its perception of the formed and changeful nature of all social life, and emphatically anti-idealist in its account of sense-making as an ordinary and practical modality of human activity as such. However, it did not claim and was not offered the franchise of Marxism. Over the next forty-odd years, this apparent indeterminacy became an obligatory topic in critical discussion. The simplest documentary evidence suggests a history in three acts: initial commitment, disillusioned withdrawal, critical re-engagement and return. Early affiliation to the cultural theory and perspectives of the Communist Party was followed, after 1945, by a phase of critical attraction to the methods and diagnosis of Leavis and *Scrutiny*, and a correspondingly distant evaluation of English Marxism. The principal early works, *Culture and Society* and *The Long Revolution*, bear the theoretical imprint of that attraction, which was not dispelled until the early 1970s, in a new phase of thought that led to the formulation of 'cultural

materialism' and Williams's self-insertion in an international community of Marxist theory. This is a plausible scheme; Williams
himself volunteered much evidence in support of it (1979: 144).
Nevertheless, it is misleading as a means of critical access to his
work, suggesting as it does a formal parallelism between the intellectual biography and the theoretical history. As in the ten-
sions of the working life, so in the logic of the theorizing:
corresponding to the engagements and disengagements of the
one, there must be shifts and breaks in the other – 'early' and
'late', 'Leavisian' and 'Marxist', or whatever descriptions taste
may prefer. The value of such interpretations is, of course, that
they underline the developing character of Williams's work over
thirty years, and the need for properly rigorous discrimination of
its character and claims. Yet it is possible to take issue with the
common versions of the narrative without lapsing into sub-
critical naivety and indulgence: to claim, as I do, that Williams's
work exhibits a fundamental continuity, yet not a fundamental
coherence. If there is a 'break' in his thinking, it is not so much a
datable, quotable intellectual-textual event as a persisting internal discrepancy. Williams's theoretical discourse is bivocal, impli-
cating 'culture' in two distinct roles.

The crux in Williams's relationship with Marxism was the tradition of cultural analysis deriving its authority from Marx's classic summary of his new-found materialist conception of history:

> in the social production of their life, men enter into definite
> relations that are indispensable and independent of their will,
> relations of production which correspond to a definite stage of
> development of their material productive forces. The sum total
> of these relations of production constitutes the economic
> structure of society, the real foundation, on which rises a legal
> and political superstructure and to which correspond definite
> forms of social consciousness. The mode of production of
> material life conditions the social, political and intellectual life

process in general. It is not the consciousness of men that determines their being, but, on the contrary, their social being
that determines their consciousness.

(Marx [1859] 1970: 181)

This formulation of the structuring role of economic relations in
the making and remaking of societies is what came to be known
and cited in the concept–metaphor of 'base and superstructure'.
Williams lodged three objections to this formula, each quite different from the others.

First, it was predictably schematic and reductionist in its treatment of concrete historical material: its determinist confidence in
regular patterns of (economic) cause and (cultural (effect) left it
unable to account fully and consistently for the typical complexity of practice and orientation in cultural formations. 'There were
industrial novels' in nineteenth-century Britain, he remarked on
one occasion, 'but what there was not was the kind of entity pos-
tulated by [Christopher] Caudwell – "capitalist poetry"'
(Williams 1979: 144). This was a familiar critical theme, a matter for rebuke and qualification in Marxist writing from the late
Engels onwards, as well as a mock-sorrowful topic for critics with
not the smallest interest in resolving the apparent difficulty.
Williams's solution – a critical development of the formula rather
than a departure from it – was to follow the disobliging indica-
tions of appearances, to affirm and eventually to theorize complexity as a normal, structural feature of cultural history. First
outlined in the closing pages of *Culture and Society* ([1958] 1961),
this understanding attained formulaic expression in *Marxism and
Literature* (1977). Any historical period was characterized by the
co-presence of three kinds of cultural formation: the 'residual',
continuing from an earlier formative period and still active; the
'emergent', taking shape in the present but tending more or less
significantly beyond its given terms; and, more powerful than either, the 'dominant', those forms and practices that most directly

assisted the reproduction of existing social relations, the bourgeois in 'bourgeois culture'.

This was a substantial issue, but not the most serious. It was, so to say, a superstructure whose misshapen features should be traced to a fault in 'the real foundation' of theory. The decisive short-coming in the base–superstructure formula was not an excess of materialism but a lack of it. In effect, Williams charged, the Marxist tradition had given priority to matter but otherwise re-tained the belief in an immaterial plane of ideas. In this way, it recapitulated the ages-old dualism of spirit and matter, inverting but not superseding its constitutive terms. This had been the general implication of his critical case against the Marxism of the 1930s, in which he identified a syncretic discourse, part economic-determinist and part Romantic idealism, the latter compensating for the explanatory weakness of the former ([1958] 1961: 271). It furnished the negative example governing the theoretical emphases of *The Long Revolution*, and eventually released the polemical energy that powered the formulation of 'cultural materialism'. The in-built suggestion of the base–superstructure formula, Williams main-tained, was that culture is a 'secondary' or 'derived' reality, an effect or expression or copy of a society already substantially con-stituted elsewhere, in relations and processes thought of as dis-tinctively 'material'. But the critique of 'natural seeing' exposed such reasoning as incoherent, as a materialism that had not yet matured into full understanding of its own theoretical implica-tions. Culture is one of the modes of creation of human reality, enjoying 'genuine parity' with them: 'It is then not a question of relating the art to the society but of studying all the activities and their interrelations, without any concession of priority to any one of them we may choose to abstract' (Williams [1961] 1965: 63,62). And given this basic parity of being, it was not clear how one kind of activity could be ceded causal privilege in the forma-tion of social relations as a whole:

[i]f we find, as often, that a particular activity came radically to change the whole organization, we can still not say that it is to this activity that all the others must be related; we can only study the varying ways in which, within the changing organization, the particular activities and their interrelations were affected.

(1965: 62)

It was possible to argue that: '[economic] production and distribution are ... essential, for the maintenance of life ... [and moreover that] the highly variable ways in which they are organized quite clearly colour our whole existence and in some cases appear to determine it' and yet to resist an 'absolute formula' (p. 62) and:

The formula that matters is that which, first, makes the essential connexions between what are never really separable systems, and second, shows the historical variability of each of these systems, and therefore of the real organizations within which they operate and are lived.

(1965: 136)

Qualified as these formulations are in regard to the question of determination by the economic, it should be apparent that Williams was not primarily concerned to write another page in the chronicle of idealist resistance to such an idea. His key critical emphases fell elsewhere. He drew attention to the internal changeability of history's constitutive 'systems', to their variable social reach and articulation. As he observed in *The Long Revolution* ([1961] 1965: 136), the relations between household production and general production (between 'the family' and 'the economy') were not constant from one form of society to another. Here, too, and again in *Marxism and Literature* (1977) and the late *Towards 2000* (1983), he emphasized the changeable social scope of 'the economic', both as a cultural category and as a systematic relationship. Furthermore – and this is what actually defines his theory, early and late – Williams insisted on the inseparability, the 'indissolubility' of 'the whole social process' ([1961] 1965: 55).

Among the three critical elements in Williams's reflections on the base–superstructure formula, this one was dominant. Not merely retained as a settled theme in *Marxism and Literature*, it was raised there to the intensity of a justifying critical passion. The most conspicuous engagements of that work – the uncharacteristically crude dealings with structural linguistics and associated Marxist styles, coming oddly from the writer who had theorized individuals as the 'bearers' of 'rules', and who, earlier and later, spoke easily of cultural 'systems' (Williams [1961] 1965: 34; Moriarty 1995) – owed a good deal of their impetus to this fundamental concern. Williams's argumentation here was typically threefold, addressing matters of substance and procedure, and also suggesting an interpretation of the theoretical difficulty. The substantive claim, that all cultural and other activities form, and function as, moments of a unitary and dynamic social process, was self-evidently in the tradition of Marx. It was distinctive mainly for its emphatically 'materialist' conception of culture and was correspondingly guarded in its concessions to the special role of the economic. However, consistent implementation of this claim depended upon rigorous control of 'abstraction', which, though necessary, threatened always to deform the substantive theory by representing analytic distinctions between cultural, political and economic modes of social life as separate spheres of reality.[1] Theory ran the risk of frustrating its own ends, and this for reasons that had less to do with procedural shortcoming than with the logic of 'the whole material social process'. Abstraction and separation were the spontaneous cultural tendencies of capitalism itself, Williams maintained. The false dissociations of the Marxist theoretical tradition, above all that of 'base and superstructure', reflected the historically specific appearances of one form of society. They were the 'fetishized' appearances, as Marx described them, of capitalism, which, as a system, fosters confusion about the objective reality of 'our common associative life' (Williams [1961] 1965: 56).

This critical association of ideas was constant: it formed the thematic core of Williams's theoretical discourse, which we may now consider in the light of a terminological curiosity. Why, even as he characterized his developed position as 'a Marxist theory', one 'within historical materialism', should he also give it a name of its own, 'cultural materialism' (1977: 5)? Both the claim and the descriptive gesture had strong, evident grounds. The terminological linkage summarized a process of theoretical struggle in which 'materialism' could come to know 'culture' adequately only by knowing itself differently, in a way more fully consistent with its own premises. Here was a theory of 'the *specificities* of *material* cultural and literary *production*' (p. 5), or, with a critical shift in emphasis, of 'the signifying system *through which necessarily* (though among other means) a social order is communicated, reproduced, experienced and explored' (Williams 1981: 13, emphases added).

So far, so convincing. Yet, there is room to inquire whether cultural materialism was simply this, whether it was no more than the theory and programme thus defined. Williams's early definition is revealing. The 'theory of culture' announced in *Culture and Society* and *The Long Revolution* was conceived as 'a theory of relations between elements in a whole way of life' ([1958] 1961: 11–12). The interest of this definition, which Williams reiterated almost verbatim in *The Long Revolution*, and again ten years later, lies in its phrasing, where an apparent redundancy conveys a decisive inflection of sense.[2] The object of the theory is not 'a whole way of life' – which, as critics have often pointed out, would be 'society', not 'culture' – but the *relations* that make it such. Culture, then, is not the whole, nor is it only coextensive with the whole. It is, rather, the principle of *whole-ness* in social life. Culture is more than a specific object of inquiry: it is the qualifying condition of all fruitful social analysis and judgement.

This was the definition of the late 1950s. Later definitions from the seventies and eighties differ significantly, in idiom and specificity of claim. Yet these differences do not validate a radical distinction between early and later Williams, between the Leavisian humanism of the one and the Marxism of the other. The later definitions redrafted but did not substantively revise the theoretical project of *The Long Revolution*, and they did not mark a break with the critical philosophical theme that counterpointed it. On the contrary, the critical function of 'materialism' in *Marxism and Literature* (1977) was to serve both simultaneously: to further the theory while sustaining a cautionary commentary upon it, and both in the name of the central category and value of the text, the 'whole'. As a qualifier of 'materialism', 'culture' was a specification but also a check: the object of a theory but also a critique of the inborn tendency of all theory in a capitalist civilization.

Valid theory, 'substantial knowledge', Williams affirmed in *The Long Revolution* ([1961] 1965: 39), was as Coleridge had defined it: 'the intuition of things which arises when we possess ourselves as one with the whole'. Unlike 'analytic knowledge', it arose from 'experience', to which, at this stage, Williams accorded special cognitive authority. The imprint of Leavisian romanticism is traceable here, but in the conceptual setting of *The Long Revolution* it is no longer so easy to interpret. Leavis rejected all theory as an obstacle to substantial knowledge, which, contrariwise, arose from the mutual possession of critic and text. However, Leavis's reasoning was dualist, in effect distinguishing valid from spurious modes of experience, one grounded in the intuition of human norms, the other a passive absorption of the dominant, 'mechanical' civilization. Authoritative experience, for him, was an exclusive universal. Williams could not, in elementary logic, appeal to 'experience' in this sense. His analysis of creativity was radically anti-essentialist, postulating experience as a historical formation of subjectivity, variable between and within societies, not a perceptual constant. And 'the human', in his discourse, marked a social principle of inclusion, not a perennial moral nature. Two other options remained. The first, which Williams took, was to abandon the criterion of experience in that dogmatic–subjectivist sense and to pursue 'substantial knowledge' within a programme of critical theory-formation. The distrust of 'analytic knowledge' persisted, sometimes emphatically, at other times less so. But as his last theoretical codifications made clear, 'experience' was to be understood as an effect of 'signifying systems'. The idea of a sovereign category of culture, 'a general concept which might be capable of indicating all [its] complex interrelations' (1981: 206), persisted too, but as a goal of theory, not a founding intuition.

The alternative was to retain the cognitive sovereignty of 'experience', but now in a historical and inclusivist perspective whose inescapable dangers would be subjectivism and relativism – the frustration of critical thought by an uncritical deference to individuals' spontaneous perceptions of themselves and their world. A passage like this, coming late in *The Long Revolution*, sees Williams exclude that option, in the name of the real categories and the theory that knows them, but then delineate, with critical ambiguity, the path by which it might return:

> In an industrial economy, social production will either be owned or controlled by the whole society, or by a part of it which then employs the rest. The decision between these alternatives is the critical decision about class, and if we are serious about ending the class system we must clear away the survivals, the irrelevancies, and the confusion of other kinds of distinction, until we see the hard economic centre which finally sustains them. With that basic inequality isolated, we could stop the irrelevant discussion of class, of which most of us are truly sick and tired, and let through the more interesting discussion of

human differences, between real people and real communities
living in their valuably different ways.

([1961] 1965: 363)

There were, in that last sentence, intimations of both the best and
the worst kinds of utopianism. Socialism is the necessary means
to a general human liberation, but, in turn, must affirm nothing
less as its historic commitment: that is the central political conviction of *The Long Revolution*. But even as he insisted on the
structural locks of capitalism, Williams echoed the terms of another discourse, one in which that 'hard' thing dematerializes
into an old and wearisome topic: 'classes' and other such categories become 'irrelevant' abstractions unworthy of 'real people'
in all their ordinary variety. Here is a kind of utopianism that
deals with capitalism by wishing it out of existence in a trans-
figuring vision of the everyday – a kind that might be called
'populist' (see pp. 134ff. below). This was not the meaning that
Williams intended and acted upon, but it was, objectively, there
to embrace, as others would. With the emergence and consoli-
dation of Cultural Studies as an organized academic pursuit,
from the later 1960s onwards, the question of populism became
crucial.

2

A CENTRE

Williams, striking beyond the discursive boundaries of Kulturkritik, explored a socialist theory and politics of culture, in the
service of a long revolution. Richard Hoggart pursued his own
critical programme in a new institutional departure, a Centre for
Contemporary Cultural Studies (CCCS). The subsequent development of critical thinking about culture in Britain – and beyond –
has been inseparable from the fortunes of that initiative, which
had no strict precedent in the record of English studies. It will be
necessary henceforward to acknowledge the new reality of collaborative academic work on culture – without, however, making
any claim to reconstruct an institutional history. What is most
important in the present context is the discursive mutation that
now occurred, in the search for an alternative collective identity
and voice. One simple way of proceeding now is to ask a question. What did Hoggart propose, and with what results?

LITERATURE AND CONTEMPORARY CULTURAL STUDIES

Hoggart's opportunity had come with his appointment, six years
after *The Uses of Literacy* (1958), to the chair of Modern English in

the University of Birmingham. The rationale and practical substance of the proposal formed the subject of his inaugural lecture.

Hoggart's title, 'Schools of English and Contemporary Society' (1970b: 245–59), testified to his continuing affiliation with the dominant national variety of Kulturkritik. His first principle was that of literary Romanticism, with its belief in the inborn superiority of literature as a mode of knowledge and judgement: 'how well would we be able to apprehend, let alone express, the complexity of personal relations, if it were not for literature working as literature?' (1970b: 248). In the implicit answer to that question lay the defining commitment of English studies. And this, in turn, implied a duty towards language in general, as the element of human discrimination, at a time when its well-being could not be taken for granted: 'I wonder whether in any previous period so many words were being used inorganically – not because the writers had something to say about their experience, but on behalf of the particular concerns of others' (p. 251).

It was not sufficient, Hoggart judged, to deplore the handiwork of 'the advertisers and the public relations men'. The ominous tendencies of contemporary usage – centrally, the human disintegration implied in the forms of public address – were systemic in kind, arising from modernity as such. They were: 'part of the price of self-consciousness (up to a point and of a certain kind), a consequence of the endlessly working conveyor-belt productiveness of modern communications, and of the increasing centralization and concentration of societies' (p. 252). To these spontaneous historical tendencies, literary criticism – the developed experience of 'literature working as literature' – was the necessary form of resistance.

Thus far, Hoggart had rehearsed the Leavisian topic of cultural emergency. But the implicit terms of *Mass Civilization and Minority Culture* were now inflected by the distinctive social commitments of *The Uses of Literacy* and a less fatalistic style of

Kulturkritik. Teachers of English would discover that: 'the voices that most readily speak to their schoolchildren are very different from the voices heard in that high art they are now trained to teach' (Hoggart 1970b: 253). And the difference was not necessarily that of the new or the antipathetic: 'many [teachers] listened to those popular voices before they came to university and some might still do so with some part of themselves' (p. 253).

'Only connect': Hoggart took over E.M. Forster's motto for *Howards End*, in urging a new effort, at once more 'humble' and more curious, to 'make sense' of this cultural 'split'.[1] 'Literature and Contemporary Cultural Studies' was Hoggart's provisional designation of this problem area, for which he outlined a field and a threefold programme of inquiry. The field would be contemporary culture as a whole: its forms, practices and organizations, the formation of its producers and of their audiences. Although there were precedents for work across so wide a field – Hoggart cited the examples of F.R. Leavis and Q.D. Leavis, 'more important than most', and George Orwell (pp. 255, 257) – it would be necessary first of all to clarify the terms of a fresh engagement:

> Talk about 'highbrows, middlebrows and lowbrows' continues, although it is now almost entirely useless as critical terminology. The education press (still following Ortega y Gasset) talks about 'your common man' and 'the masses' as though these were well-defined terms rather than conditioned gestures. Most of the discussion of conformity, status, class, 'Americanization', mass art, pop art, folk art, urban art and the rest is simply too thin.
>
> (1970b: 255)

Critical review, 'historical and philosophical', of 'the cultural debate' would therefore inform the second aspect of the studies, which would involve empirical research in the sociology of contemporary culture, its writers, artists and audiences, its circuits of authority and reputation, its underlying economy, and their myriad 'interrelations'. The third, and the 'most important', form of inquiry would be literary criticism. There were strong methodological reasons for this ordering of priorities, Hoggart maintained. Only 'the directly literary critical approach', with its developed practices of rhetorical and thematic analysis, could determine the specificity of textual phenomena: 'unless you know how these things work as art, even though sometimes as "bad art", what you say about them will not cut very deep' (p. 257).

Claims of this kind are valid enough, but, paradoxically, only within limits that Hoggart's discursive tradition refused to accept as compatible with an adequate apprehension of literature. Literary 'art', in the Leavisian school of English and contemporary cultural studies, bore witness to the possibility of human wholeness. Literary criticism realized itself only in so far as it understood this, and was thus not so much an analytic 'approach' as an indispensable control on all purposeful cultural inquiry. This was the problematic of English Kulturkritik, which had governed the reasoning of *The Uses of Literacy*, and which, the inaugural lecture made plain, retained its primordial authority in Hoggart's discourse. But it was a problematic no longer perfectly in place. The reference to Orwell was a local sign of a disturbance in cultural identification and vision. Among the many things that students of popular culture needed to learn, Hoggart suggested, was 'a little more humility about what audiences actually take from unpromising material'. Indeed: 'perhaps no one should engage in the work who is not, in a certain sense, himself in love with popular art'. If it was true that 'one kind of "love" is a disguised nostalgia for mud', that 'assimilated lowbrowism is as bad as uninformed highbrowism', it was also true that in the ambiguities of mass art and in the ambivalent experience of it there was insight to be gained:

All this is related also to hopes, uncertainties, aspirations, the search for identity in a society on the move, innocence, meanness, the wish for community and the recognition of loneliness. It is a form of art (bastard art, often) but engaging, mythic and not easily explained away.

(p. 257)

Even in its 'increasingly machine-tooled' forms, 'there are sometimes spaces between the brittle voices in which a gesture sets you thinking in a new way about some aspect of human experience.' In short, 'we have to recognize the meaningfulness of much popular art' (pp. 258–9).

The valorization of literature as the touchstone of moral sentience, the representation of modern history as a spontaneous process fostering abstraction, indifference and disintegration, the answering strategy of engagement with the contemporary, in a trans-disciplinary effort governed by literary criticism: Hoggart varied these characteristically Leavisian perceptions and commitments in the direction of greater openness and curiosity, but, unlike Williams, did not try to displace them. At the same time, he could not simply re-enact the characteristic social gesture of Kulturkritik, the drama of minority significance versus mass stimulus and response. In acknowledging the 'meaningfulness' of 'much' popular culture, he implicitly called into question the ascribed identities, faculties and relations of the discourse as such, the constitutive terms of its claims to authority. But this disturbance – eased already by that saving 'much' – was a sign of strain, not a moment of rupture. The cultural identity of 'we' and the status of 'meaning' remained awkward in Hoggart's own work. Was popular culture 'meaningful' only as 'symptom', or could it be 'representative', not merely expressing but exploring and criticizing its conditions of existence? Was a faltering paternalism the only alternative to 'the new populism'? (Hoggart 1970a: 205–8)

These questions were left at the boundary of Kulturkritik to be taken up in the new Centre for Contemporary Cultural Studies.

FROM HOGGART TO STUART HALL

Without Richard Hoggart there would not have been a Centre. But the inspirational figure in the history of the CCCS, the individual who did more than any other to fashion its character, was Hoggart's deputy and eventual successor in the role of Director, Stuart Hall. Of course – and who has not learned to say so? – this is problematic. For here was a 'centre' that did not or could not or must not embody any of the qualities that the metaphor suggests. It was not a fixed point or even a singularity. It did not regulate a boundary or determine a path towards closure. It was not the origin of Cultural Studies, or its end. Philosophical glosses of this kind, which are conventional in retrospects of Birmingham, are motivated as much by honour as by conviction. A comparative institutional history, integrating anecdote and archival material in a wider politico-cultural context, would be illuminating. But for the purposes of a less ambitious account, it can be said that if Stuart Hall cannot be taken to represent the Centre, then it cannot be represented at all.

Hall himself has never spoken for the CCCS quite as, to take a relevant comparison, F.R. Leavis, with all the usual disclaimers, would speak for *Scrutiny*. Diversity, openness and provisionality are the recurring themes of his various reconstructions – which form the greater part of the published record (Hall 1980a; 1996c). His writings from the Centre – frequently authored with others – highlight a practice of 'negotiation' (one of his key words) with critical interlocutors both inside and outside the institution. This was not only the sign of a certain working context. His post-CCCS writing in the eighties and nineties has shared with the early work a habit of strong, punctual emphasis but also, quite generally, a tendency to elusion. Systematicity is not a positive value for Hall, who explicitly distinguishes 'Theory' from his own preferred practice of 'theorizing' (Hall 1996a: 150). In his case, then, as much as in that of CCCS, there is reason for critical caution, but also, perhaps, for a little compensating tenacity. For Hall's work is highly thematic, and if it has no use for fixed schemes, its propensities are nevertheless quite regular.

Hall was exceptionally well-qualified to implement the idea of a Centre for Contemporary Cultural Studies. He had been trained in English literature, in Jamaica and later at Oxford, and then gone on to develop working interests in film, television and mass literary forms. His first professional publications were an essay on film studies and a book, co-authored with Paddy Whannel, *The Popular Arts*.[2] He had been a founding member of the New Left, one of the team that created *Universities and Left Review* and the first editor of its successor, *New Left Review*. His characteristic emphasis within these collectives was not merely the contemporary – the necessary orientation of any political commitment – but the new. His earliest political essays pursued the apparent novelties of Britain in the fifties, a remaking of Conservative politics and – controversially – an emerging 'sense of classlessness' (Hall 1958). And, like Hoggart or Williams though more decidedly so, as a black subject of the Empire, he had not inherited and could not simply assume an unmarked intellectual identity in England's dominant culture. There was, in this personal combination, the ground of continuous development from scheme into practice and cumulative achievement, but there was also the potential for a leap forward – which is what happened in the unimagined conditions of post-New Left culture in the later 1960s. Hoggart set his course by the natural lights of English Labour politics and a modified cultural liberalism. Hall, who had been formed in the 1950s crises over Suez and Hungary, espoused a more radical socialism and a general principle of renewal, both in politics and in theory, where Marxism seemed to him an inescapable, though also questionable, affiliation. With all institutional and personal considerations set aside, Hall's interests were far better adapted to the emerging culture of the left. The easing of Cold War ideological pressures, the intensification of anti-colonial and anti-imperialist warfare throughout the non-metropolitan world, and the structural expansion of higher education in conditions of faltering capitalist prosperity were the formative conditions of mass student radicalism in the major countries of the West. The events of May–June 1968, when a student revolt in Paris sparked a general strike of French workers, the escalation of the wars of liberation in Vietnam and Cambodia, and the international wave of solidarity they inspired, were the most spectacular manifestations of the new phase. The British student insurgency was modest in scale, duration and striking-power, but it was one necessary condition of a cultural remaking of the left. The other condition was more strictly intellectual. These were the years of *New Left Review*'s 'Western Marxist' programme, through which Hall's successor editors worked to displace the dominant traditions of socialist thought in Britain – an 'empiricist' indifference or hostility to theoretical inquiry and a characteristically 'English' confidence in the virtues of piecemeal social reform. With its mightily self-possessed liberal intelligentsia, accommodated labour movement, and weak, compromised Communist Party, Anglo-British culture seemed especially resistant to radical attack. *New Left Review*'s conviction was that systematic, critical dissemination of Europe's unofficial Marxist schools would assist the formation of independent and versatile socialist thought in the homeland of 'empiricism'. Some of this work was already available in English, but only a concentrated effort of learning and discussion could unlock the critical potential of the tradition as a whole (Anderson 1976; *New Left Review* 1977). The year 1968 dates the symbolic fusion of politics and ideas, the entry of a new intellectual generation into popular struggle and a spring tide of revolutionary criticism in the bourgeois academy. In the same year, Hoggart left Birmingham for Paris – on secondment to UNESCO – and Hall assumed undivided responsibility for the Centre.

TEN YEARS OF CULTURAL STUDIES

Looking back, just over a decade later, in the last days of his tenure, Hall judged that Cultural Studies had achieved autonomy, now having 'a direction, an object of study, a set of themes and issues, a distinctive problematic of its own' (Hall 1980a: 26). Its project was 'the elaboration of a non-reductionist theory of cultures and social formations' (pp. 39–40). How far did this conception honour Hoggart's prospectus of 1963, and how far did it deviate from it? CCCS had remained committed to *the contemporary*. Its principal interest lay in that 'period of change and development' that had opened with the 'qualitative break' or 'decisive rupture' of the Second World War. Although it had come to define its working chronological range as one hundred years (from 1880), the Centre maintained its emphasis on contemporaneity as the presence of the new. However, the range of *the cultural* had now been expanded. In Hoggart's definition, the repertoire of cultural forms was effectively bounded by the law of copyright, including published works and licensed performances of all kinds, but not, apparently, anything more. The majority population, now glimpsed as culturally active, yet non-producing in this sense, came into sociological vision as audiences. The organizational and economic relationships he proposed to investigate were, implicitly, those of cultural commerce. The Centre amended the sociological brief through a process of critical reflection that also transformed the core definition of the field. Public as well as commercial institutions were drawn into range: BBC television news broadcasting, for example, and the formal education system, including its literary curricula. Ethnographic initiatives, mainly in the controversial field of youth 'sub-cultures', which CCCS explored as 'rituals of resistance', brought the central structures of state and economy into critical question and at the same time confirmed Hoggart's audiences as producers in their own right, collective authors of the texts and performances of everyday life.³ Cultures – the plural was now inherent in the definition and thus implicit in any use of the singular – were now understood 'anthropologically' (Hall) as ensembles of practices, not primarily as artefacts, high or low, to be analysed in abstraction from their economic and political conditions of existence.

But what, then, would be the distinctive pattern of cultural *studies*? Hoggart, while urging an opening to sociology, had been at pains to emphasize its intrinsic inadequacy to the object of inquiry: literary criticism alone could furnish the means of elucidating the operations of culture as such. He had also urged a critical audit of conceptual resources, as part of the effort to capture the defining 'interrelations' of contemporary culture as a whole – a 'philosophical' priority not inevitably favoured by the ethnographic emphasis on self-interpreting experience (Hall *et al*. 1980: 88–95). Indeed, both requirements had been met, though in forms that hardly matched the expectations of 1963. The specificity of culture as a mode of social practice came to be reasoned from premises quite alien to the English literary-critical tradition. Structuralism, a theory–method generalized from Saussurean linguistics and instanced, in the work of the CCCS, by Claude Lévi-Strauss and Roland Barthes, grounded a conception of culture as 'signifying practice', an active and structured making of sense. The analytic programme so authorized was at once inclusive, coherent and specific. It acknowledged meaning as coextensive with sociality. It saw in any signifying practice, irrespective of its place in the order of social distinction, the same general process of selection and combination of terms and relations from an already-given code. It also gave analytic priority to forms, or, in Hall's words (1980a: 30), shifted attention 'from the *what* to the *how* of cultural systems'. In all three respects, the structuralist option seemed an advance. Yet, it could only be a moment in a more comprehensive theoretical development. As a radically anti-expressive theory of signification, according priorities to codes over messages, structures over meaning-events, it was not self-evidently reconcilable with strong conceptions of autonomous cultural agency, of individuals and groups as active creators of their world. Moreover, the inner logic of structural analysis pressed towards formalism and abstraction, bracketing meaning and dismantling society – and thus draining the Birmingham project of its sense, which was precisely the exploration of the social order of meaning. Social theory proper, an account of 'interrelations', was a necessary interlocutor, and above all a corpus of theory whose signal importance for CCCS was its characteristic preoccupation with 'questions of culture, ideology and "the superstructures"', in a style 'consciously counterposed to the vulgar reductionism of the Marxism of the Second and Third Internationals' – the 'base and superstructure' reasoning which was taken to have dominated official Marxist theory from the 1880s to the present (1980a: 25).

Two theorists had special impact: the French philosopher Louis Althusser and the Italian Communist thinker Antonio Gramsci. Althusser, with his insistence on the necessary complexity of the social whole, on the 'relative autonomy' and 'specific effectivity' of all social practices, outlined one possibility of a non-reductionist account of 'cultures and social formations' (Althusser 1969). His concepts of 'overdetermination', which identified the presence in any given social relation of the other relations forming its conditions of existence, and of 'conjuncture', the unique state of overdetermination that defined this complex social whole at any given moment, opened the way to historical as well as theoretical specificity in analysis. Gramsci, to whom Althusser owed significant debts, had pioneered the study of culture as a mode of political struggle, as the site and means of the effort to establish, or resist or counter, the non-coercive rule of dominant class blocs, their 'hegemony', the historical 'common sense' that secures the actual 'consent' of the oppressed – and this always in historical, 'conjunctural' forms of analysis (Gramsci 1971). These were the chief exemplars of 'an open Marxism' capable of going beyond dogmatic reiteration to discover something new (Hall 1980a: 29).[4] Of course, 'the break into a complex Marxism' meant continued attention to its inherited problems, above all, the unresolved concept of 'ideology', which would now have to be thought in relation to the emerging concept of 'culture', and, underpinning these – or dominating them – the old vexation of 'base and superstructure', which Raymond Williams had made a central theoretical issue (CCCS 1978; Hall 1980b). More gravely, perhaps, it remained an open question whether Marxism, as a general theory, could actually survive the discovery of something new. The feminist 'interruption', as Hall termed it, had already challenged the primacy conventionally accorded to class relations in the formation of social consciousness, and invalidated the associated reduction of 'material conditions' to 'exclusively economistic or "productivist"' terms (Hall 1980a: 38; 1996c: 268; Brunsden 1996). The question of race was already interrupting both (CCCS 1982; Gilroy 1988). Dogmatic appeals to classes, their essential interests and necessary struggles, were inadequate to the political, theoretical and moral challenges posed by the subordination of women, and the weighty and complex psycho-social reality of gender. A cultural theory that could not account for the central modern experience of racism, and for the universal reality of ethnicity, would be stunted. Nevertheless, Hall maintained, the problems, if not the familiar solutions, of Marxism were the crucial ones for a materialist 'theory of cultures and social formations'. They were 'the heart of the matter' (1980b: 72).

THE NEW SUBJECT

Gramsci's lessons were theoretical but also ethical and political. Hoggart had suggested that the new subject area called for a different kind of subjectivity, meaning by this a modified balance of sympathy, a willingness, at last, to 'connect' with popular cultural life. Under Hall, the Centre pursued a more radical aim, seeking not so much to modify the typical identity and address of Kulturkritik, the social relations inscribed in its discourse, as to displace them, in 'a new kind of intellectual practice' and a corresponding 'organizational form' (Hall 1980a: 43). Collectivism was the governing norm of CCCS activity. Its members organized themselves into working groups – devoted, say, to media or women or race – but also participated in regular plenary sessions, where particular projects were opened to wider discussion, in a general context of urgent, often hard-fought theoretical development. The Centre *Working Papers* were thematically co-ordinated, and favoured joint, often multiple authorship – practices that survived the journal's mutation into a fully commercial series of books. These forms of organization had an inherent intellectual value. They helped to strengthen irregular cross-disciplinary initiatives against the spontaneous resistance of the entrenched division of academic labour, by promoting an ethos of mutuality in research and criticism. They were consonant with the anti-individualist style of the left in the seventies, and, specifically, implied the will to discontinue the run of charismatic performances that had defined the historical personality of Kulturkritik. Their most general rationale was political, emerging from a distinctive reading of Gramsci's strategic reflections on the social dynamics of intellectuals (Gramsci 1971: 5–14). On the one hand, as Hall put it, there were the 'traditional' intellectuals, who typically 'set themselves the task of developing and sophisticating the existing paradigms of knowledge'. On the other, there were

> those who, in their critical role, aim to become more 'organic' to new and emerging tendencies in society, who seek to become more integral with those forces, linked to them, capable of reflecting what Gramsci called 'the intellectual function' in its wider, non-specialist and non-elitist sense.
>
> (Hall 1980a)

The role of this kind of intellectual was, first, to engage critically with modern ideas 'in their most refined form' (Gramsci) and to do so, Hall would subsequently add, 'without theoretical limit'; second, to contribute to 'popular education', to communicate beyond the quasi-natural boundaries of established intellectual life. 'Our aim', he declared, 'could be defined as the struggle to form a more "organic" kind of intellectual' (Hall 1980a: 46).

Hall emphasized the difficulty and necessary modesty of this ambition. The objective social order of knowledge could not be cancelled by an act of will, and intellectual self-reform yielded contradictions of its own (for example, collectively written texts might, by virtue of their process of composition, be less, not more widely accessible). Nevertheless, the ambition was inherent in the project of Cultural Studies at Birmingham. It seemed impossible to dissolve the *object* of Kulturkritik, to re-imagine mass civilization as a space of meaningful popular choice and activity, without also dissolving its *subject*, the authorized voice of the cultural principle. '[To] produce work which is progressively more "organic" ... has been, throughout, the Centre's task and goal' (Hall 1980a: 47).

3

A THEATRE OF CRITICAL SITUATIONS

Stuart Hall's association with the Birmingham Centre is so evidently important in any account of his work that its relatively short duration may be overlooked. It lasted some fifteen years in an intellectual career that began in the middle 1950s, and it preceded the decades of his greatest productivity and influence as a cultural theorist and engaged intellectual of the left. That unfinished record of activity demands attention in its own right.

Hall's formative critical relationship was with the New Left – which had been peripheral to Richard Hoggart's vision – and with its inspirational intellectuals, Raymond Williams and Edward Thompson. In this perspective, his parting account of the CCCS in the 1960s and 1970s appears differently. Hall narrated a theoretical journey in three stages, beginning with resources of literary-critical and historical provenance, continuing as a struggle in and against sociology, and then, with crucial assistance from structuralism, emerging into the open space of a 'complex Marxism'. There is no reason to query this account of a sequence of studies. Yet, as the history of a problem it seems circular, in as much as the questions that were put to sociology were already those of the complex Marxism that lay beyond it, and indeed had formed the initial endowment of the Cultural Studies project. A complex Marxism – or better, an emphatically 'complex' relation to Marxist tradition – was inscribed in its genetic code, which regulated a peculiarly 'organic' interdependency of theory and politics.

HALL: BEYOND NEW LEFT 'CULTURALISM'

In a second retrospect, this one conceptual rather than institutional, also published in 1980, Hall gave this formative relationship much greater prominence (Hall 1980b). Together with Hoggart, he confirmed, Williams and Thompson had 're-founded' the study of culture. In *Culture and Society*, Williams had 'settled accounts' with the anterior tradition (p. 58).[1] *The Long Revolution* assigned a fundamentally different theoretical content to the old terms, positing 'active and indissoluble relationships between elements or social practices normally separated out. ... "Culture" is not *a* practice. ... It is threaded through *all* social practices, and is the sum of their interrelationship' (Hall 1980b: 59). In developing this conception, moreover, Williams had resisted

> the literal operation of the base/superstructure metaphor, which in classical Marxism ascribed the domain of ideas and of meanings to the 'superstructures', themselves conceived as merely reflective of and determined in some simple fashion by the 'base'; without a social effectivity of their own. That is to say, his argument is constructed against a vulgar materialism and an economic determinism.
>
> (Hall 1980b: 59–60)

Thompson's *Making of the English Working Class* had taken its shape in a distinct but comparable pattern of critical engagements – here, with economic and labour history, and with English Marxist historiography – with convergent results: 'in its foregrounding of the questions of culture, consciousness and experience, and its accent on agency, it also made a decisive break: with a certain kind of technological evolutionism, with a reductive economism and an organizational determinism' (Hall 1980b: 58). That is to say, it broke with any theoretical scheme that converted popular self-expression into a ventriloquistic effect of machinery, economic 'laws' of motion, or party enlightenment.

At the same time, nevertheless, Thompson had found fault with Williams's distinctive historical emphases, in a critique that became a standard reference in Cultural Studies. *The Long Revolution* was misguided, Thompson argued, in its emphasis on culture as 'a whole way of life' — a pacific, evolutionist notion to which he counterposed the more dramatic 'whole way of struggle'. And there was a counterpart abstraction of 'power' and of culture as 'ideology', the familiar Marxist notion of socially motivated misrepresentation, which Thompson glossed as 'a *system* of ideas and beliefs, a constellation of received ideas and orthodox attitudes, a "false consciousness" or a class ideology which is more than the sum of its parts and which has a logic of its own' (Thompson 1961).

Hall seconded these objections, which seemed to identify a political insufficiency in Williams's cultural theory, but then went on to define a critical perspective in which both Williams and Thompson appeared open to challenge. The difficulties of the 'culturalist' paradigm, the category to which he now assigned *The Long Revolution* and *The Making of the English Working Class*, were both theoretical and political. 'Culturalism' opposed the relegation of the cultural to the role of economic after-beat, the secondary, merely superstructural reflex of a 'real' material world: 'it conceptualizes culture as interwoven with all social practices; and those practices, in turn, as a common form of human activity: sensuous human praxis, the activity through which men and women make history' (Hall 1980b: 63). However, culturalist forms of analysis won their release from economism at the cost of another kind of determinism, which Hall characterized in the manner of Louis Althusser:

> in their tendency ... to find common and homologous 'forms' underlying the most apparently differentiated areas, their movement is 'essentializing'. They have a particular way of understanding the totality – though it is with a small 't', concrete and historically determinate, uneven in its correspondences. They understand it 'expressively'.
>
> (1980b: 64)

This tenacious embrace of the whole as a whole was, in the first instance, a theoretical difficulty. It inhibited the attempt, which Hall judged indispensable to cultural theory, 'to think *both* the specificity of different practices and the forms of articulated unity they constitute' (p. 72). And further, in so far as it accorded a privileged role to 'experience', it obscured the action of structuring relations in the force-field of history. In this way, it promoted a 'naive humanism', with 'the necessary consequence': a political practice that was 'voluntarist' in its estimate of the historical potency of will and 'populist' in its deference to spontaneous popular self-consciousness (p. 67).

Hall's counter-move, a critical traverse of 'structuralism', was designed to correct the apparent shortcomings and aberrations of the 'culturalist' paradigm, but not to reject its questions. These he assimilated to his own thematic, a cluster of theoretical and political meanings that regulated his own complex relation to Marxist discourse on culture. Some appropriately general, synoptic discussion of that relation will be necessary, but it will be helpful to approach it with renewed awareness of Hall's specific, concrete engagements in the years since the 're-founding' of cultural discourse. Three cases may serve, if not as epitomes then at least as illustrations and occasions for critical pause. One is from the 1970s, accentuating issues in cultural analysis (media discourse). A second is from the 1980s, contrastingly political in matter and address (the new course of capitalism and its subjects). A third, setting the emphasis of the 1990s, is involved with questions of identity (the cultural politics of ethnicity). In Hall's movement through these fields of engagement, a certain narrative unfolds itself: not, to be sure, a well-made plot, rather a sequence in the (theoretical) life of the subject.

THE STRUCTURES OF SIGNIFICATION

Television has been the epicentre of cultural disturbance since its general development in the mid-twentieth century. It was the main concern of Hall's work in the early 1970s, and an exemplary case for his most general positions in cultural theory. *Encoding and Decoding in the Television Discourse*, which was first aired in 1973, outlined a whole orientation in critical research.[2] Hall's purpose was to theorize televisual communication as a specific signifying practice, a structured social relationship in the domain of meaning; to argue that audiences played an active part in this discursive process, which, though structured and thus constraining, was not guaranteed in its effects; and to show, in terms that were neither technical nor psychologistic but social, how 'distortion' entered the circuit of meaning. In an Althusserian paraphrase, his purpose was to think both the 'autonomy' of a cultural practice and its structural 'relativities'. Following a methodological indication in Marx, Hall characterized communication as a structured process in which 'no moment can fully guarantee the next moment with which it is articulated'. The whole so formed is truly 'complex' rather than 'expressive', in that none of its elements can simply be reduced to any other. However, in as much as the process is specifically communicative, 'the discursive form of the message' is dominant. An 'event' must become a 'story' before there can be a '*communicative event*' (Hall 1980c: 129), and the story, the representation that is the sense of the latter, must be intelligible within 'the frameworks of knowledge' of the audience. 'Encoding and decoding' are the constitutive activities of the process, which can thus no longer be grasped as the optimal transmission–reception of pre-given 'content'. Hall's generic theoretical reference here was structural linguistics, but his discussion of 'connotation', the second-order significations that cluster around the 'literal', denotative meaning of the sign, called upon more probing and socially engaged semiotic styles – those of Roland Barthes (in *Mythologies* and the earlier, anti-structuralist V.N. Vološinov (*Marxism and the Philosophy of Language*).[3] Connotation, for Hall, was the presence of history in even the most literal image:

> The level of connotation of the visual sign, of its contextual reference and positioning in different discursive fields of meaning and association, is the point where *already coded* signs interact with the deep semantic codes of a culture and take on additional, more active ideological dimensions.
>
> (Hall 1980c: 133)

It was the level at which the sign was 'open to new accentuations and ... enters fully into the struggle over meanings – the class struggle in language' (p. 133).

The corollary of this claim was that the indeterminacy of connoted sense was itself determinate. While connotative codes were typically less clearly and less strictly defined, they were '*not* equal'. They functioned in 'a *dominant cultural order*' in which 'the different areas of social life appear to be mapped out into discursive domains, hierarchically organized into *dominant or preferred* meanings'. Since this order was 'neither univocal nor uncontested', preferred meanings could not be guaranteed. But in so far as it was dominant, it underwrote a balance of probability, favouring the preferred readings and limiting the range of deviations from them: 'Of course, there will always be private, individual variant readings. But "selective perception" [the official account] is almost never as selective, random or privatized as the concept suggests.'

Decoding activity exhibited 'significant clusterings', for which Hall, concluding, proposed a formal Gramscian typology of viewing 'positions': the *dominant–hegemonic*, the *negotiated* or *corporate*, and the *oppositional*. In the first position, the viewer works within the dominant order of connotation, so producing the 'ideal' experience of communication (the national interest is the national interest). In the second, 'adaptive' and 'oppositional' codings intersect: the hegemonic order of meaning is honoured, yet suspended for an 'exceptional' case (the national interest demands general pay restraint but my own union's claim is justified). The third position involves deliberate, critical recoding in an alternative order of meaning (for 'national interest' read 'capitalist interests'). The discrepancies between the first and second positions were the real condition of 'misunderstandings' and 'failures of communication', Hall suggested. The passage from the second to the third, should it occur, was a moment of crisis: 'Here the "politics of signification" – the struggle in discourse – is joined' (1980c: 138).

Hall's essay enacted a post-'culturalist' turn in advance of its formal designation. 'Culture' was now secured as a strong modality of social relations, one implicitly coextensive with social life itself, and as a field of active popular (and other) subjects. However, the primary purpose of the analysis was to establish the autonomy and productivity of specific cultural practices – in this case, television – and at the same time to explore their structured relations with the society as a whole. The meaning of the cultural practice would not be 'guaranteed' as the 'expressive' moment in social relations. It was itself materially structured work. Yet contrary to pluralist or populist belief, audience activity was not unconstrained. Production and reception alike were subject to the ordered probabilities of an englobing dominant culture, which encoded determinate conditions of economic and political existence. The field of culture was worked over by ideology. Summarized in these general terms, Hall's essay cleared a path beyond the perceived obstacles and hazards of 'culturalism', leading towards a Marxist theory and politics of culture. In another, later essay, however, his reasoning seemed to point in the opposite direction. The paradoxical occasion of this reverse was a plea upon behalf of the new.

NEW TIMES FOR SUBJECTIVITY

New Times was the name of a project of political reconstruction forwarded in the 1980s by a group of modernizing Communist intellectuals and non-party collaborators. The institutional base of the project was the party monthly, *Marxism Today*, in which Hall's political writing had become a signal feature. Hall contributed to the New Times discussions, and, with the journal's editor, Martin Jacques, assembled the book-length version of it. The core thesis of New Times was economic. Capitalism was now undergoing a major internal reorganization involving a transition from the 'old assembly-line world of mass production' and mass markets to a new world of 'flexible specialization' and product differentiation – or in the standard terminology, from a 'Fordist' to a 'post-Fordist' regime of accumulation. This change was not 'exclusively economic ... in the narrow sense'. Post-Fordism was 'shorthand' for a comprehensive remaking of society and culture:

> The 'New Times' argument is that the world has changed, not just incrementally but qualitatively, that Britain and other advanced capitalist societies are increasingly characterized by diversity, differentiation and fragmentation, rather than homogeneity, standardization and the economies and organizations of scale which characterized modern mass society.
>
> (Hall and Jacques 1989: 21, 11)

The urgent task now was to impress this reality on a political left that preferred old 'certainties' to 'venturing into uncharted territory', so much so that it had become, in many ways, 'a culturally conservative force' (p. 14). This was the context of Hall's synoptic version of New Times.

Hall disavowed the totalizing ambitions of culturalism or mechanical reductionism. 'New Times', he wrote, signified 'an attempt to capture, within the confines of a single metaphor, a number of different facets of social change, none of which' – post-Fordism, post-industrialism, postmodernism or 'the revolution of the subject' – 'has any necessary connection with the other' (Hall 1989: 117). The post-Fordist thesis itself was 'not committed to any prior determining position for the economy'. But strong metaphors live dangerously, and this one had totalizing, determinist ambitions quite its own. The contemporary historical process, as Hall rendered it, appeared integrated, directed, and fateful in its implications for the old 'mass' society, its economy, politics and culture. Post-Fordism was reinventing a whole world, one for which Hall found his descriptions in the analytics of Michel Foucault and Jean-François Lyotard's vision of a 'postmodern condition' relieved of 'grand narratives'. Post-Fordism was the matrix of an expanded and 'pluralized' civil society, with enriched possibilities of choice in everyday life. In the new conditions, 'the all-encompassing state' no longer dictated the range and the forms of political engagement. Politics was now coextensive with civil society, where 'points of power and conflict' multiplied, and now encompassed matters hitherto deemed 'apolitical' – the family, health, food, sexuality, the body. There was no 'overall' map of this new situation, but perhaps no conventional need for one either. 'Perhaps there isn't, in that sense, one "power game" at all, more a network of strategies and powers and their articulations' (p. 130). Politics, long thought to move in concert with the 'economic', was now contrastingly 'cultural' in bent, in keeping with the general tendency of 'the revolution of our times' (p. 128). For

[if] 'post-Fordism' exists, then it is as much a description of

cultural as of economic change. Indeed that distinction is now quite useless. Culture has ceased (if it ever was – which I doubt) to be a decorative addendum to the 'hard world' of production and things, the icing on the cake of the material world. The word is now as 'material' as the world.

(p. 128)

The old distinction between 'objective' and 'subjective' moments of change no longer held, Hall continued, and subjectivity itself had turned mercurial. The familiar collective subjects – those of class, nationality, ethnicity, gender and so on – were becoming 'more segmented and "pluralized"', as the individual grew more salient, and subjectively more mobile and various, in a culture that celebrated self-fashioning and promoted the aestheticization of the everyday. Much of this culture might be 'commodified consumption', but to halt at that familiar judgement was to miss its historic promise: the 'democratization' that 'is *also* potentially part' of 'the hidden agenda' of market exchange, and 'the opening up of the individual to the transforming rhythms and forces of *material* life' (p. 128).

This lesson on New Times was addressed to 'the left', a formation contrastingly 'old' in its resistance to their meaning. Of the counterpart 'old times', the world of states and class struggles once evoked as the englobing reality of the television audience, not many traces remained. Although Hall and his co-editor stressed the corrective point in their monocular framing of the present – exaggeration as a necessary critical tactic – that intention does not adequately account for the pattern of Hall's mode of address or his governing theme. In an interview given some two years earlier, Hall had spoken with fine, mocking feeling against elitist expropriations of popular speech, which none the less continued to have disruptive historical force: 'it is as if the masses have kept a secret to themselves while the intellectuals keep running around in circles trying to make out what it is, what is going on' (Hall [1986] 1996b: 140). The kind of intellectual 'politics' he had in mind was that 'which follows from saying that the masses are nothing but a passive reflection of the historical, economical and political forces which have gone into the constitution of modern industrial mass society' (p. 140).

This characterization emerged in the course of a discussion of postmodernist theorizing, but its reference is critically more general and ambiguous. It might describe Kulturkritik, and might serve equally as a chilly reference to Marxism. An associated phrase citing 'false consciousness' and 'the banalization of mass culture' as negative equivalents corroborates the impression that, in a certain perspective, 'the left' could seem little more than a sub-set of 'the intellectuals'. This association, in so far as it takes hold, produces an overall adjustment of categories and a counterpart association between 'the masses', or popular subjects, and the prevailing social order, on the ground of 'reality'. Here, arguably, was the discursive logic of New Times as a whole, and of Hall's keynote essay, which, as it were, unveiled the 'secret' that eluded 'the left'. This form of address was not itself new, or merely the creature of a polemical occasion. It had characterized the cultural writings of George Orwell, who systematically counterpointed popular secrets to left-intellectual doctrine, in this way authorizing his own habit of heresy. It became the call-sign of Cultural Studies practitioners, intellectuals who in less cranky ways also thought to become 'more organic'. Orwell's secret reality was a traditionalist Englishness, and thus antithetical to Hall's commitment to the modern and the hybrid. But the secret pleasures of everyday capitalism, which Hall now disclosed to the left, were not less ambiguous as cultural grounds for a critique of politics, and no less serviceable for a more up-to-date kind of populism.

Hall exaggerated the novelty of the times, in the interest of accentuating the discrepancy between the real world of popular modernity and the genre narratives of left tradition. However, the function of the 'new' in his discourse was not merely descriptive.

More than a contingent quality (present or not, exaggerated or not) of social phenomena, it seemed to be an index of their relative value, and, in a further elevation of significance, a necessary condition of worth, to be ascribed where it could not simply be found. Thus, in a passage already cited here (p. 116 above), he over-wrote his not-so-old objection to 'culturalism', asserting that the culture/economy distinction was 'now' obsolete. Culture had 'ceased' to be a 'decorative addendum', he announced, though a disarming parenthesis owned up to his general theoretical conviction that it had never been such. 'The word is now as "material" as the world' – that is to say, as much as it had always been. Another passage, also concerning the social status of the cultural, exhibited the same tendency to convert logical into temporal relations: 'There is no clear evidence that, in an alternative socialist economy, our propensity to "code" things according to systems of meaning, which is an essential feature of our society, would *necessarily* cease – or, indeed, should' (Hall 1989: 235). This is a logical bluff. If the 'propensity' really is 'essential', the possibility of cancelling it cannot arise, and appeals to the balance of evidence are redundant. Hall's compulsive temporalization of logic, which grants to discursive shifters like *now* and *no longer* the status of truth-tests, is symptomatic of a perspective in which novelty has become a value in itself and even an autonomous cultural force.

This valorization of the new was not part of the break towards cultural studies, much though that involved engagement with the contemporary. It was a constant in Kulturkritik, and, in the more activist varieties of that discourse (Leavis's, for example), a practical rationale. In those cases, of course, the value of the new was negative: it was a 'portent' or a manifest danger. Tradition was the positive term, not, as it effectively became for Hall, Marx's incubus that 'weighs like a nightmare'. That polarization establishes the distance between Hall's text and those earlier manifestos for new times, but also illuminates the form of their

antagonism, which was symmetrical. F.R. Leavis saw a technological apparatus, not a mode of production, as the engine of modernity. Hall acknowledged capitalism, but gave analytic priority to
specific regimes of production and consumption – Fordism and
its emerging successor.[4] Leavis relegated politics to the status of
administration, an instrumental practice without final significance. Hall dispersed the political, in the sense of a system of
practices enmeshed with state and government, 'generalizing' it
as the instance of struggle in an expanded civil society. Both saw
the new forms of labour-process as decisive for popular life, but
with opposite emphases and valuations. Leavis deplored 'standardization and levelling down', while Hall privileged the potential of the new 'rhythms of material life'. Against the automatism
of 'mass civilization', Leavis upheld the critical value of 'minority
culture', the historic commitment of an intelligentsia strong in
its intuitions of essential human purposes, but now largely
stripped of its moral authority or tempted to trade its responsi-
bilities for reputations. Hall validated the spontaneous tendencies
of the post-Fordist everyday, and strained to force them to the attention of a left now isolated in its traditionalist dogmas. New
times, strange times. Hall is no Leavisite – the thought is
grotesque – but in this socialist manifesto he replicated the discursive form of that 'old' recusant discourse, rewriting Kulturkritik
in a mirror, as futurism.[5]

IDENTITIES IN MOTION

The idea of native virtue was shared ground for Orwell and
Leavis. Orwell's populist socialism took its nourishment from the
intuition of a continuous, normative Englishness, as did Leavis,
whose humanist elitism rested its claim to authority on the en-
dowments of a national popular past. Neither variety of cultural
reason could have resolved the paradoxical idea of 'new ethnicities'. This plain phrase, which indicates the dominant theme of

Hall's writing in the 1990s, activates a whole unfinished history of aspiration and blockage. Ethnicity, in common understanding, is never new. Like the genes and the gods, it is for all time. And the pluralization of the term imputes variousness in a domain where relationships are least of all relative: character and tradition are fate. Hall's case, broached in the context of black cultural politics in Britain today, told against all such perennialist and essentialist commonplaces, with critical implications of the most general kind (Hall 1996d).

Hall distinguished two phases in the recent history of black cultural engagement (the immediate occasion was a London seminar on Black Film and British Cinema, though the horizon of implication lay well beyond that). In the first, the values of political colour – 'black' as the signifier of convergent histories and a shared situation – claimed priority over diverse identifications of ethnicity and race. The leading practice was to challenge the positioning of blacks as 'the unspoken and invisible "other"' of the dominant (white) aesthetic and cultural discourses. The goal was access to the sites and means of cultural production, for the purposes of affirmative self-representation, against the grain of the dominant, racist order of signification. That kind of cultural politics continued, and must do so indefinitely, Hall maintained. However, in a second phase of struggle, one was no longer concerned only with the 'relations of representation', initiative was passing to 'the politics of representation itself', to a theory and practice of culture beyond 'the innocent notion of the essential black subject' ([1989] 1996d: 441–3). Representation was now grasped as 'formative' and 'constitutive', not 'expressive'; and the shaping conditions of 'blackness' would now appear as historical, without 'guarantees in nature'. Hall's definition of ethnicity carefully sieved the concept to eliminate any trace of literal or metaphorical genetic purism: just as 'black' had been sprung from racist discourse and remade as a positive term, so now 'ethnicity' must be reappropriated from mainstream multiculturalism, which tended to absolutize it as changeless cultural personality. Ethnicity was 'what acknowledges the place of history, language and culture in the construction of subjectivity and identity', and, more than that, 'the fact that all discourse is placed, positioned, situated, and all knowledge is contextual' (p. 446). The vagueness of this formulation disconcertingly conveyed its critical positive assertion. Ethnic identities are not fixed by inheritance. Rather, they form and re-form in successive and varied contexts of existence. *Diaspora*, a great scattering of populations across oceans and continents, had been a distinguishing condition of black cultural history, which thus recorded a pattern of encounters between acquired resources and the expectations, demands and possibilities of new situations − a complex sequence in which, however, there was no plausible option of 'return'. Ethnicity thus marked the permeability of 'race' in its constitutive relations with the orders of class, gender and sexuality, which were never fixed in a quasi-natural scheme of essences and characters. Conversely, the self-differing differences of ethnicity must now be seen as universal, no less a feature of national populations and classes that claim unmarked universality than of those they subordinate, and in doing so mark as 'ethnic'. Ethnicity did not so much characterize the actors in cultural politics as delineate the field and object of their struggle:

> We still have a great deal of work to do to *decouple* ethnicity, as it functions in the dominant discourse, from its equivalence with nationalism, imperialism, racism and the state, which are the points of attachment around which a distinctive British or, more accurately, English ethnicity has been constructed. ... We are beginning to think about how to represent a non-coercive and a more diverse conception of ethnicity, to set against the embattled, hegemonic conception of 'Englishness' which, under Thatcherism, stabilizes so much of the dominant political and cultural discourses, and which, because it is hegemonic, does not really represent itself as an ethnicity at all. ...
> Fifteen years ago [in the seventies] we didn't care, or at least

> I didn't care, whether there was any black in the Union Jack.
> Now not only do we care, we *must*.
>
> (Hall [1989] 1996d: 447–8)

Hall's concept of ethnicity had no part in the cult of genes and custom that the term familiarly evokes. Maintaining a strong contextual association with 'race', integrating relations of class, gender and sexuality as elements of its core definition, it was nevertheless irreducible to any of these categories – or, indeed, to itself.

Ethnicity here played a performative role, fulfilling, in its definition, Hall's standing principles of historical specificity and uncertainty. It could not be schematized, without self-cancellation; more than any other social category, it embodied contingency – that which is neither necessary nor impossible. However, there were corresponding political risks in this 'positive conception of the ethnicity of the margins, of the periphery', with its 'politics of ethnicity predicated on difference and diversity' (Hall [1989] 1996d: 447). It might serve to reinforce the postmodern populism into which New Times had been tempted, or – Hall himself noted – might slacken into something not very different in effect, a revised liberal pluralism. As it happened, the logic of his critique of the notion of 'the essential black subject' led him to reverse the emphases of his New Times essay, to affirm the stolen freedoms, the moment of carnival, in popular culture, but also to insist upon the structuring realities of symbolic subordination and the capitalist market:

> popular culture, commodified and stereotyped as it often is, is not at all, as we sometimes think of it, the arena where we find who we really are, the truth of our experience. It is an arena that is *profoundly* mythic. It is a theatre of popular desires, a theatre of popular fantasies. It is where we discover and play with the identifications of our own selves, where we are imag-

ined, where we are represented, not only to the audiences out there who do not get the message, but to ourselves for the first time.

(Hall [1992] 1996g: 474)

The language of this passage, with its syntactic shift from active to passive voice ('we discover ... we are imagined') and its crucially equivocal diction ('we are represented ...'), draws a fine but firm line between the popular and the populist.

However, a more general problem remained, as Hall was aware. What, or where, was the 'politics' in this 'cultural politics'? Discounting as inadequate an unbounded liberalism of 'difference' – 'an infinite sliding of the signifier' – he nevertheless acknowledged the apparent difficulty in his own cultural position, which

does not make it any easier to conceive of how a politics can be constructed which works with and through difference, which is able to build those forms of solidarity and identification which make common struggle and resistance possible but without which political contestation is impossible, without fixing those boundaries for eternity.

(Hall [1989]1996d: 444)

In a subsequent talk on the same topic, this one more pronouncedly critical of the old black essentialism, Hall reiterated his conviction that 'there *is* a politics to be struggled for', and gave an illustration of its concerns and rationale. Endorsing Paul Gilroy's contention that 'blacks in the British diaspora must, at this historical moment, refuse the binary black *or* British', he explained:

You can be black *and* British, not only because that is a necessary position to take in the 1990s, but because even those two terms, joined by the coupler 'and' instead of opposed to one

> another, do not exhaust all of our identities. Only some of our identities are sometimes caught in that particular struggle.
>
> (Hall 1996g)

This reasoning – on behalf of a demand that is itself compelling – indicated a path of theoretical advance but also incarnated the obstacle laid across it. Politics is not coextensive with culture, nor is their relationship stable over time. Yet in so far as this distinction is drawn in the plane of 'identities', it is liable to fading, or simple erasure: politics as a motivated disturbance in and of the identity-complex that is culture, and not ostensibly anything other than that. Hall had admitted 'the difficulty of conceptualizing' the politics he now urged, but it may be that the real difficulty arose from the conceptualization already in place – a 'cultural politics' in which the critical accent had quietly slipped back from the second (and secondary) term to the first.

WRESTLING WITH MARXISM

Of the many critical dialogues that give Hall's work its individual texture, the most sustained and most agitated has been with Marxism. The recurring issue has been the determining role of economic relations in culture and politics, 'that old base/superstructure paradigm' ([1986] 1996b: 135). But as that old phrasing should suffice to remind us, some things are too obvious to be altogether visible. Here, as in the prior case of Williams, it is worth asking just what was at stake. In fact, Hall's constructive theoretical purpose was closely akin to Williams's. He had two related aims. The first was to establish the specificity of culture as a constitutive social practice in its relations with the other constitutive practices, political and economic, of the social as a whole. The second was to develop forms of analysis capable of grasping the concrete historical shapes of these relations in their irreducible originality. The base–superstructure formula seemed inadequate to this task. It was reductionist, appealing to mechanistic or expressivist notions of causality that read culture as the effect of a more fundamental activity or as the emanation of a core reality, and in either case consigned it to a passive, second-order existence. Its privileged reality was the economy, and specifically its objective system of classes, whose forms of subjectivity were assumed to be fixed at that level. Third, it was necessitarian, dogmatically committed to discovering only what it already posited as the inevitable state and direction of affairs. Hall's first critical appeal was to Louis Althusser, who rethought the formula in terms of a necessary complexity of structure, proposing an 'overdetermined' totality of relatively autonomous social practices, which the economy determined only 'in the last instance'. Althusser's theoretical reconstruction assigned analytic priority to 'the conjuncture', the concrete, unrepeatable state of this complex whole in a given space and time. However, his own work remained at a higher level of abstraction, and did not resolve the ambiguities of 'the last instance'. Antonio Gramsci, on the other hand, had fashioned his conceptual instruments in and for his analyses of a concrete historical society, Italy, and it was on his work that Hall based his own canons of inquiry: not 'capitalist society' in general but capitalist 'social formations' (Britain) and their unique 'conjunctures' (Thatcherism); not generic 'classes' but 'historic blocs', specific formations of classes and other social forces; not 'the dominant ideology' pure and simple but the much more complex matter of the prevailing 'common sense' and the struggle within it for non-coercive social authority, or 'hegemony' (Hall [1986] 1996c).

The most salient characteristics of this Marxist variety were its valorization of culture as a site and modality of political struggle, and its strategic emphasis on 'the concrete situation'. Two reorientations in general theory insured them against the stunting effects of 'orthodoxy'. Pursuing his critique of expressive causality, Hall rejected 'economic determinism' in favour of a conception of 'determinancy' in which the economic appeared not as a cause, in the stronger sense of that term, but as the shaping environment of 'thought':

> The determinancy of the economic for the ideological can ... only be in terms of the former setting the limits for defining the terrain of operations, establishing the 'raw materials', of thought. Material circumstances are the net of constraints, the 'conditions of existence' for practical thought and calculation about society.
>
> (Hall 1996a: 44)

The notion of conditions that constrain, and, in that strong yet imperfect sense, determine thought – a notion owing something to the later Williams – was compatible with the base–superstructure paradigm (Williams 1977: 87). However, Hall was inclined to associate it with a theoretical break towards a new understanding of culture, in which rival forces struggle, within the unbounded, practically infinite space of language or languages, to fix the order of meaning. These struggles over meaning are the specific (residual) reality of 'ideology' – the instance of political desire in language, as it were – which, therefore, can no longer be understood as an 'expression' of preconstituted social subjects. It is rather an 'articulation', in Ernesto Laclau's word, a linking of discrete social meanings such as 'people' and 'nation', a conjoining of 'elements which do not in themselves have any necessary political connotations', and in which subjects find positions of utterance and agency (Hall [1993] 1996h: 295, 305).

This, by the early 1990s, was Hall's consolidated alternative to that old base–superstructure paradigm. But what precisely did it displace? Not a generic theoretical reality called Marxism, even though he had entertained the designation 'post-Marxist' and characterized his relations with the tradition as 'wrestling with the angels' (Hall [1986] 1996b: 148; [1992] 1996e: 265).

Neither was it, in any simple sense, the conception of determination by the economic, notwithstanding the frequency of his reproaches over many years. Hall's style of engagement with this familiar crux is worth particular attention. Speaking of the theoretical challenge posed by feminism, for example, he announced: 'a break with any residual attempt to give the term "material conditions" an exclusively economistic or "productivist" meaning' and underscored '[the] necessary complexity of different kinds of contradiction, attributable in neither a "first" nor a "last" sense to the "economic" in its simple designation' (Hall 1980a: 38). Some years later, referring directly to Marx and his theoretical tradition, he repudiated 'the automatic conception of classes lodged at the heart of fundamentalist Marxism', and insisted that ideas 'do *not* precisely mirror, match or "echo" the class structure of society' (Hall [1986] 1996c: 423, 434).

The shared stylistic feature of these formulations is their thickness of modification. Adjectival phrases, inverted commas and variant repetition make up a good part of their substance, and with paradoxical effects. These modifiers add force to the utterance but at the same time obscure its exact propositional content. Only discursive convention inhibits the recognition that the criticism is more vigorous in its address than it is clear in its conceptual reference. The last of these four instances exhibits the rhetorical pattern with special vividness, strenuously denying what no serious interlocutor would assert, but also adding a modification ('precisely') that, taken seriously, would reduce the drama to bathos. Emphasis, in cases such as these, is the opposite of what it purports to be: it is a way of not coming to the point. It is the deceptive figure of theoretical evasion. The meanings of Hall's quarrels with the old paradigm are not the stereotypes they often seem.

A stable set of preferences has governed Hall's critical orientation in the field of Marxist theory. Wherever there appears to be a tension between objective conditions and subjective discretion, or between the general and the specific, or between the abstract and the concrete, he favours the latter term. His privileged object of analysis is the *conjuncture*. His cardinal value, ethical as well as cognitive, is *contingency*, the 'openness' of history as site and practice. There can be no self-consistent Marxist objection to these tenets, in general terms: they are the necessary presuppositions of any project of historical inquiry and purposeful action. Yet it may be judged that in Hall's discourse they exercise more than the necessary minimum force, supporting a distinctively voluntarist appreciation of historical processes. Gramsci proposed a distinction between the 'organic' elements of a concrete situation – its 'relatively permanent' constitutive features – and the 'conjunctural', those elements that 'appear as occasional, immediate, almost accidental'. The reality of the situation, he said, lay in its specific configuration of the two, in their 'dialectical nexus', which analysis must attempt to capture, however difficult the task (Gramsci 1971: 177–9). In Hall's usage, the conjunctural achieves clear, constant priority over the organic, which, in turn, undergoes a tendentious redefinition. Thus, he could criticize appeals to 'the logic of capital' in cultural studies – to the structures and propensities of capitalism as formative realities of contemporary culture – on the grounds that 'very little by way of concrete and conjunctural analysis can be derived at this high-level … form of abstraction' (Hall 1980b: 71). The interest of this judgement lies not so much in its intentional claim as in the default assumption that the 'concrete' and the 'conjunctural' are equivalents. This is questionable. For Gramsci, the conjuncture is a moment in the longer organic life of a social formation, which is no less concrete for being more extensive in time. But Hall assimilates the concrete to the conjunctural, in opposition to the organic, which is now reduced, via the ambiguous category of 'the capitalist epoch as a whole', to the 'abstraction' of a mode of production as such. In this way, he effectively suspends the operation of the 'relatively permanent' aspects of historical situations,

to the advantage of what is 'occasional, immediate, almost accidental' in their formation, and thus, ironically, lends credence to
an abstract valorization of the present-as-possibility – the 'voluntarism' for which he rebuked Williams and Thompson. His practical sense of *contingency* respects the same deep preference. The
contingent is what is neither necessary nor impossible. It is one of
the basic philosophical assumptions from which historical analysis
sets out, not a meaningful guide to any particular substantive
conclusion. It specifies nothing about what is surely crucial in any
given concrete situation, namely, its discoverable order of *probabilities*. But once the constitutive action of 'the organic' is suspended,
contingency emerges as the simple and sufficient conceptual other
of necessity, as pure electivity, in a historical field where low probabilities enjoy a paradoxical enhancement of opportunity.

Hall would almost certainly reject this as a position in cultural
theory, even if he were to acknowledge it as what I claim it is, an
objective propensity in his thought. Its logic is in a way existen-
tialist, prompting the thought that the work of Jean-Paul Sartre
may bulk larger in his intellectual inventory than has commonly
been noticed. Its political motivation is more familiar. The error
that Hall has struggled to expunge from Marxist cultural theory
is not generic 'determinism' but the specific form of it known,
since Althusser, as expressivism – the notion that social phenomena
are so many transcriptions of an essential economic principle. In
practice, his concern has been still more specific, or rather selective, emphasizing not so much 'the economy' in its totality as the
associated system of classes, and not the totality of such relations
and interests but rather the working class, with its structurally
given attributes and goals. Illustrated in this setting, expressivism appears as something worse than a theoretical error: its
logic of explanation constitutes a *de facto* denial of popular creativity, the very principle of cultural studies. By the 'popular',
Hall wrote at the turn of the 1990s, he and his collaborators in
CCCS had meant 'those forms and practices which are excluded

from, and opposed to, the "valued", the canon, through the operation of symbolic practices of exclusion and closure' (Hall [1993] 1996h: 293). He recalled how, in their work on sub-cultures, they had pondered: 'the built-in limits to all such forms of resistance – because of their gestural quality, their dissociation from the classic agencies of social transformation, their status – as it was put in the language of the time – as "magical solutions"' ([1993] 1996h: 293). His retrospective comment is telling: 'This is a serious question ... but this way of putting it also reflected the lingering presence of the belief that the symbolic could not be anything but a second-order, dependent category' ([1993] 1996h: 294).

It is indeed a serious question, and just as serious, in its own scale, is the fallacy in Hall's interpretation of it. A 'second-order, dependent' practice is by definition incapable of transforming the social whole that includes it, But it does not follow that first-order practices are equivalent in their capacity to do so. The unexamined possibility remains that practices may be equally material – and in that sense co-primary – and yet unequal in their power to constitute and reconstitute social relations, and this precisely because of their material specificity as practices. The terms of the old anxiety, as Hall reports it, acknowledge this possibility. His interpretive retrospect denies it, confusing an interesting question of political theory – what is the strategic weight of cultural practices? – with that old topic of economic reductionism. In a moment such as this one, the critique of the base–superstructure appears as something more than the scientific pursuit it can legitimately claim to be. If Hall's attacks on economism seem compulsive, excessive in relation to their long-discredited object, it is because they serve a wider strategic purpose, one long familiar from the reasoning of Kulturkritik. The insistence on the material effectivity of culture, its first-order reality, also plays an allegorical role in a ritual affirmation of its political capability, its claim to social authority.

Hall has more than once reminded an audience that the cultural binary high/low, although lacking essential grounds of any kind, retains its considerable historical efficacy. The warning is apt, and not least in relation to his own work. The propensities of his 'complex Marxism' – a certain futurism, voluntarism and cultural reduction of politics – are the signs of a discursive otherness within it, elements of the uncanny, attesting the continuing force of Kulturkritik, which has been renounced, negated, turned upside down and inside out, but not quite overcome. It would be wrong – inaccurate and unjust – to represent them as the essential truth of Hall's theorizing. It is difficult to annotate them without exaggeration – though when Ortega wrote that exaggeration is a necessary condition of thinking at all, he was exaggerating only slightly. It is proper to acknowledge that these propensities find their sustenance in real and grave problems: how to manage the permanent difficulty of being contemporary; how to estimate the strategic force of the symbolic, in a society in which culture is commodified, commodities are eroticized and political authority depends upon popular consent. Yet, it is necessary to recognize their reality and force, and the discursive ambivalence they betoken. Hall's writing is at least as complex as he would wish. Dialogue, for him, is a principle of individual style. The great cast of interlocutors his prose assembles is in that sense the opposite of Hoggart's chorus. Yet that chorus has not left the stage, and appears at times to lead the dialogue as a whole. The possibilities of Cultural Studies are nowhere so richly illustrated as in the work of Stuart Hall, and this is among them.

4

TOWARDS POPULAR CULTURE?

Kulturkritik was (and is) amateur. Spoken more often than not from academic sites – in literary studies above all, but also in sociology and philosophy – it nevertheless remained an elective, committed practice, a tendency driven by logics of love and hate. Cultural Studies, likewise but oppositely committed, has evolved into a profession, with all the opportunities and entailments of its academic kind. The proliferation of this tendency–discipline on the campuses of the English-speaking world and beyond has favoured the most noteworthy recent development in its common intellectual life: by the middle 1990s, it has been estimated, one in every four new Cultural Studies titles was about Cultural Studies itself (Ferguson and Golding 1997: xiv–v). Some of these writings continue long-running disputes over theory and method in the field – over the relative validity of explanatory and interpretive strategies of analysis, for example, or the different varieties of ethnographic research (Garnham 1997; Morley 1997; McGuigan 1992). Some, in keeping with the first impulse of the discipline, argue the claims of unrecognized cultural subjects, seeking not merely to enlarge the field of inquiry but to reorder it: gender and race were historic 'interruptions' (Hall) of this kind, and the postcolonial thematic has since emerged as a more or less radical revisioning of both. Textbooks and course readers make their predictable, growing contribution to this literature of self-representation, but only to generate as much anxiety as they are designed to moderate, since they fuel the demand for self-definition that Cultural Studies habitually resists. As Richard Johnson has written, perhaps consciously defying the lesson of Mickey Mouse, the sorceror's apprentice in the Disney classic *Fantasia*, Cultural Studies is properly 'a process, a kind of alchemy for producing useful knowledge; codify it and you might halt its reactions' (Johnson 1996: 75).

'Institutionalization' – the inscription of an autonomous project in a formal education system – is among the darker themes of the collective autobiography. It has been overwritten, in the 1990s, by the larger, more portentous narrative of 'globalization'. Both are regularly invoked in the current phase of self-examination, as Cultural Studies practitioners look to their constitutively 'political' beginnings and ends, commitments that must not be scanted in the new environments of production and circulation (Mellor 1992). Yet these reference points are hardly secure. 'Birmingham' has been decentred, in a fractious international network now conventionally resistant to all claims of origin, especially where they concern an old colonial heartland. That tradition is specifically British – English, even – and not a template for others, in Australia or the Unites States, say, who affirm the distinct, more or less contemporaneous, beginnings of their own cultural studies (Carey 1997; Frow and Morris 1993; Stratton and Ang 1996). Ends are not self-evident either, in a period in which the great emancipationist projects of modernity are said to have lost coherence and authority, and not so much for ill as, in all senses, for good. The story of an academic quarterly is perhaps emblematic. In the middle 1980s, *The Australian Journal of Cultural Studies* gave itself into the care of a London publishing corporation. It was decided that the leading editorial role would henceforward rotate from Australia to Britain to the United States and so around again. A less limiting address now seemed appropriate, and the journal was re-launched shorn of all locative indication as *Cultural Studies*. In 1991, a further simplification occurred: editorial roles were stabilized, and assumed by two US academics, Lawrence Grossberg and Janice Radway. This was the second time in a year that Grossberg had taken the rostrum in the general interest of his discipline. With Cary Nelson and Paula Treichler, he had organized the huge international 'Cultural Studies' conference at the University of Illinois (1990). Its edited proceedings, published under the same title in 1992, have been perceived as an attempt not merely to illustrate but to *be* the discipline — a mock-international forum incarnating 'a new American hegemony in English-speaking cultural studies' (Jameson 1993; Stratton and Ang 1996: 363–5). At *Cultural Studies* the journal, meanwhile, the new editors' first visible act of policy was to rewrite its politico-intellectual charter. Marxism and feminism disappeared as tokens of past or future affinity in the new declaration, which, with admirable inclusiveness, committed Cultural Studies to the front lines of equal-opportunities liberalism.[1]

POPULISM IN CULTURAL STUDIES

By this time, and in the perceived conditions of a new world order in Cultural Studies, the anxious themes of depoliticization and intellectual decline had become familiar — in the United States as well as in the old capital, Britain, where the 'American' development fed apprehension, in Canada and in 'postcolonial' Australia (Barker and Beezer 1991; Ang 1992: 311–21; Hall [1992] 1996e: 273–5). By this time, too, a more closely defined polemical theme had won equally widespread sponsorship. Often motivated by the same anxieties, this was in any case quite distinct in its implication: the danger now manifest in the discipline was not depoliticization but active political misdirection. Cultural

Studies was developing backwards, into 'populism' (Williamson 1986: 14–15; Modlewski 1986; Craik 1987; Birch 1987; O'Shea and Schwartz 1987; Morris [1988] 1996).

What's in a charge? Populism, for all its attachment to the great simplicities of people and nation, is often confusing as a political phenomenon (some would say, always and essentially so), and its definitions are correspondingly unsettled. Its varieties have extended from left to extreme right. It has framed the strategies of peasant revolutionaries, as in late-Tsarist Russia, and militant trade-unionists, as in Argentina more recently. It has also been turned against the working class, as it was in Margaret Thatcher's Britain, and as it is now turned against blacks and other *Ausländer* in the inflamed nationalist sub-cultures of the European Union. The populism at issue in the more modest case of Cultural Studies is unquestionably of the left, by lineage and declared affiliation. In the Marxist tradition, the designation 'populist' has normally conveyed a critical judgement on strategies that mistakenly – or wilfully – subsume working-class interests under a wider and putatively common cause, which may be more or less pronouncedly 'national', but is invariably that of 'the people' and its (unique) culture. Varieties of that kind of populism have had a role in post-war Labour and Communist history in Britain, and also, as Stuart Hall and others have judged, in the thinking of the early New Left, but with little independent effect (Anderson 1980; Williams 1980: 233–51). 'The nation', in Anglo-British politics, has long been the discursive property of the dominant class bloc. The left has never gained access to it in fundamentally oppositional terms (though Orwell stands as an illustration of the desire to do so). Most who claim it today are fighting rearguard actions in the name of presumptions and destinies now officially suspended: bigoted monoculturalists, Westminster Unionists and Europhobes. 'The people', in the relevant, expanded sense, have been no easier to rally. In a country with an old capitalist agriculture, historic priority in industrial production and high levels of concentration in commerce, small property has been culturally indistinct and politically weightless: where the ordinary folk are not bonded as 'the nation', they pass unobtrusively among the great wage-labouring majority.

However, small intellectual networks are more impressionable than whole societies, and the Birmingham tradition – which, emerging from the New Left, is a specific formation of that Labour-cum-Communist culture – has not escaped charges of populism on both 'national' and 'popular' grounds. The first term of the indictment is politically the more urgent, in a quite concrete sense. The meanings of 'Englishness', inevitably though not exclusively in its association with 'Britain', have become critical in the two generations since 1945, and will be integral to the cultural politics of the next two, as 'national' (ethnic and constitutional), European and global relations assume unprecedented shapes. For now, nevertheless, the relevant past is no more resolved than the future. Paul Gilroy, himself a graduate of the Birmingham Centre, has insisted on the implausibility of efforts to winnow 'good' from 'bad' English nationalism – to quarantine a domestic popular tradition from the overseas history of a slaving, colonizing state, which was the real strategic context of nation-formation – and denounced the persistence of nativist assumptions in early New Left discourse (Gilroy 1988; 1992). There are good grounds for Gilroy's criticism, which has been widely accepted – in one case by a commentator who, disconcertingly, accepts the evidence but reverses the verdict, dismissing the criticism as ill-conceived (Carey 1997: 16). Englishness was a condensing moral–social value in Edward Thompson's writing, and also in that of Hoggart, whom Williams, himself a principal suspect in the matter, took to task for just this reason. The work of Raphael Samuel, who was, like Thompson, a historian, a rebel Communist and a key presence in the early New Left, lends further weight to this consideration, while also complicating it. Yet there may also be reason in the arguments of those who claim that British cultural studies emerged as a critical element in the post-imperial crisis of national identity. Some draw attention to the presence of ethnically marginal figures – Williams, for example, and Hall – in its formative years (Schwartz 1989: 250–5). Others are willing to venture that the British case may illustrate a general rule of emergence for cultural studies, one that has perhaps held good for Australia and the United States as well (Stratton and Ang 1996: 381–8).[2] The arguments in the first group have not been concluded; the evidence in the second seems insufficient; neither testifies to a fatal implication in the idea of the nation. Indeed, the stronger temptation, in the great conversation of *fin de siècle* academia that is home to Cultural Studies, is that hasty and simplified notions of globalization and the local, or an overgeneralized resort to the idea of postcoloniality, will foster the illusion of a new post-national condition and a corresponding inattention to the continuing force of the nation-state in the patterning of large- and small-scale social relations today.

The second charge, bearing on 'the popular', has much greater plausibility, but for reasons that enjoin caution rather than confidence in critical evaluation. The imputation of nationalism has come, unambiguously, from the left. It is a moment in the conflictual development of an emancipatory cultural politics in the sphere of race and ethnicity. The issue of populism has been posed in this sense – but also, earlier and with greater resonance, in the interest of a more familiar and better-established cause. There is, after all, a perspective in which any positive interest in the culturally popular must be suspect: that is, the perspective of Kulturkritik. For a Leavisian, for example, the claim to find values where there can only be prices, to see activity and choice where history dictates passive uniformity, is self-evidencing populism of the most reprehensible kind. If Kulturkritik is not what it used to be, its topics retain their intuitive appeal to the common sense of academia and polite journalism. The wisecracks about the structural analysis of beermats, or mock-heroic rallies championing, say, Keats over Dylan, can still charm the educated crowd. Such talk, in the forums of properly critical dialogue, has the value of rhubarb. The popular, as it has been taken up in Cultural Studies, is not a simple transvaluation of 'the mass', nor is it the locus of some 'authentic' alternative to it. No essential formal property distinguishes its genres and practices as 'low' rather than 'high'. Although it has been involved in these categorizations, which have real effects and therefore cannot be excluded in the interests of conceptual purity, popular culture has come to be seen, as it was for the authors of *Resistance Through Rituals* (Hall and Jefferson 1976) as: 'those forms and practices which are excluded from, and opposed to, the "valued", the canon, through the operation of symbolic practices of exclusion and closure' (Hall [1993] 1996h: 293). It is, if not necessarily oppositional, at least 'subaltern' in Gramsci's sense: its relevant contrary is not 'high' or 'minority' but 'dominant' (Shiach 1989). This conception is the shared ground of the controversy, not the encampment of one party to it.

Indeed, the keyword, 'populism', has itself been claimed on both sides. For Judith Williamson and Meaghan Morris – two early critics of the rising trend – it is a plain negative. For Iain Chambers, whose version of the popular has been central to the dispute, it is affirmative. Jim McGuigan's title, *Cultural Populism*, defines the field of his critical labour, not his thesis, which in fact depends on a distinction within the category. His opening definition is a problem in itself: 'Cultural populism is the intellectual assumption, made by some students of popular culture, that the symbolic experiences and practices of ordinary people are more important analytically and politically than Culture with a capital C' (McGuigan 1992: 4). Sliding, at the crucial point in its elaboration, into the conversational usage of Cultural Studies – the self-validating appeal to what is 'politically important' and the facile reference to 'Culture with a capital C' – this might be either parodic or complicit or both. In any case, it is not the inclusive characterization the argument calls for. However, a little further elaboration relieves the ambivalence: 'The vital point is to do with the *positive relationship* between intellectuals and popular culture [which includes] an appreciative non-judgemental attitude to ordinary tastes and pleasures' (1992: 4). Thus, Stuart Hall and Raymond Williams are representatives of a 'left-democratic populism' (1992: 26), as indeed is the Labourist Kulturkritiker Richard Hoggart, who imagined the Cultural Studies practitioner as humble and a little in love. McGuigan himself is a cultural populist in this sense. The case he has to make concerns an *'uncritical* populist drift in the study of popular culture, a discernible narrowing of vision and fixation on a self-limiting set of issues' (1992: 5) – against which he upholds 'the possibility of a *critical populism*' that might unify interpretive and explanatory forms of inquiry, accounting 'for *both* ordinary people's everyday culture *and* its material construction by powerful forces beyond the immediate comprehension and control of ordinary people' (1992: 5).

In effect, McGuigan charges, Cultural Studies began by mobilizing the concept of 'the popular' against the elitist image of 'the mass', but has since tended to conflate the two, finding in the forms and practices of the culture industry the conditions of autonomous popular activity (1992: 38). Valorizing the spontaneous pattern of cultural recreation in this way, uncritical populism is not simply naive, it is objectively conformist. Banal routines are transfigured, becoming deceptive modes of subversion. Television and shopping are now revealed as sites of dual power: 'there is so much action in the micro-politics of everyday life that the Utopian promises of a better future, which were once so enticing for critics of popular culture, have lost all credibility' (1992: 171).

McGuigan has been reproached – by John Storey, for example (1996: 7–8) – with misrepresenting Cultural Studies as a monolith. The claim is unfair, most readers of his book will judge, but it is also in part self-defeating, for it carries the necessary implication that his charge as he actually states it has grounds in reality. It is possible to judge that McGuigan exaggerates the incidence of the problem, and to query his belief that the solution lies in a renewed intellectual association with critical political economy, and yet to acknowledge that this is so. And indeed, such acknowledgement is not merely widespread in Cultural Studies. In one form – which Storey himself illustrates – it has become a conversation-piece in the discipline (Storey 1996: 7). The journal *Cultural Studies* carried two anti-populist texts in its first issue, and soon afterwards published Jim Bee's challenge to the 'First Citizen of the Semiotic Democracy' (1989: 353–9). Ien Ang – herself charged with populism by Tania Modlewski – has stressed her differences with 'the most exuberant ambassador of this position', who has 'virtually declar[ed] the audience's independence in the cultural struggle over meaning and pleasure' (1996: 242–3). Angela McRobbie – who figures in McGuigan's shortlist of pop conformists – mocks the claims for 'hyperactive' audiences and disowns 'the few wilder voices who see self-expression and resistance residing in the actions of those who loiter in shopping malls' (1996: 256). Meaghan Morris has discerned in the phenomenon of Cultural Studies fandom a new persona: 'the white male theorist as bimbo' (1996: 159). All these sarcasms refer to one individual: populism is multiform, legion, and its name is Fiske.

John Fiske has certainly worked for his professional notoriety. In a book such as his *Television Culture*, the complex relations between 'containment' and 'resistance' in viewing experience undergo euphoric simplification, and the audience takes control of the broadcast text (Fiske 1987; 1996: 115–46). Or, in words borrowed from the French cultural theorist Michel de Certeau, 'the strategies of the powerful' are ceded no advantage over 'the tactics of the weak' (Morley 1997: 125) – an estimate that in most real-world situations would guarantee defeat. Yet, as McGuigan and others have pointed out, Fiske does not in fact occupy a paradigm apart (McGuigan 1992: 75; Barker and Beezer 1991: 12). The rule of perverse optimality that governs his readings – that is, the less probable interpretation is normally the more compelling one – is widely respected, if not often so rigorously observed, in Cultural Studies. Even Stuart Hall, whom McGuigan exonerates on the principal count, could mistake a big-hearted pop concert for a 'movement'.[3] There is perhaps an element of ritual in this collective willingness to isolate Fiske, which suggests that the group may feel more threatened than it cares to say. Meaghan Morris's critique of 'banality in Cultural Studies' – a text widely cited, though not often with a due sense of disturbance – is indispensable here. Her 'bimbo' trope is deadly: cruel indeed, but also critically incisive. What is at stake in the matter of cultural populism is not only – not even mainly – a sentimental or wishful valorization of the popular cultural object; it is the discursive fashioning of the subject who claims to represent it.

BIMBOS AND FANS

The 'banality' that Morris perceives is that of the bad 'mass' object of Kulturkritik. It has been reanimated now, she argues, as the authentic posture for the practitioner of Cultural Studies. The return has specific practical effects: 'Once "the people" are both a source of authority for a text *and a figure of its own critical activity*, the populist enterprise is not only circular but ... narcissistic in structure' (Morris [1988] 1996: 158, emphasis added). Escape from 'the circuit of repetition' is conceivable, Morris believes, but the familiar alternative option in the discipline is 'to project elsewhere a mis-understanding or discouraging Other figure (often that feminist or Marxist Echo, the blast from the past) to necessitate and enable more repetition' (p. 158). Morris here spotlights some key features of the Cultural Studies performance: the convention of self-justification, associated with an equally conventional refusal of self-definition; the trope of an adventure forever only beginning; the thirty-something will to be young at heart. But the bimbo-subject is not only narcissistic; it is also mindless. Feminism ('grumpy') and Marxism ('cranky') are residues of a pre-postmodern ethic of critical reason, which Iain Chambers, another of Morris's case studies, has renounced in favour of a new theory or format of knowledge, what he calls a 'popular epistemology'.

For Chambers, popular culture is not only a field of activity and of committed inquiry; it is the space of a democratic alternative to the dominant forms of knowledge. He writes: 'Official culture, preserved in art galleries, museums and university courses, demands cultivated tastes and a formally imparted knowledge. It demands moments of attention that are separated from the run of daily life' (Chambers 1986). Popular culture, the everyday experience of a late-twentieth-century city, shapes a different kind of 'expertise', one that

> mobilizes the tactile, the incidental, the transitory, the expendable; the visceral. It does not involve an abstract aesthetic research amongst privileged objects of attention, but involves mobile orders of sense, taste and desire. Popular culture is not appropriated through the apparatus of contemplation, but, as Walter Benjamin once put it, through 'distracted reception'.
>
> (Chambers 1986)

The 'public is an examiner', Chambers concludes, in words borrowed from Benjamin, 'but an absent-minded one' (1986: 12). The novelty and special value of its kind of critical intelligence is that it is the opposite of the familiar kind. Here is a protocol for the Cultural Studies subject – though 'studies' hardly describes the format of engagement that Chambers offers to exemplify in *Popular Culture*. No more meta-discourse: to seek to explain the passing scenes of popular culture 'would be to pull them back under the contemplative stare, adopting the authority of the academic mind' (1986: 13). Such 'vanity' ignores the epistemological promise of ordinary distraction: 'an informal knowledge of the everyday, based on the sensory, the immediate, the pleasurable and the concrete' (1986: 13).

The selection implicit in this general description of popular culture is as tendentious as Eliot's list from 1948 – the cabbage, the Derby and the rest (see p. 55 above). It is, of course, contemporary in implied sensibility, and in that respect the opposite of Eliot's: Chambers's pastoral belongs to the street. But it presses strategically in the same direction, and even more strongly. Chambers's everyday is, rather more fully than Eliot's, the simple other of 'high' culture and its associated faculties: fast food and dance are its likeliest epitomes, and any popular interest calling upon a different order of investment becomes a practical self-contradiction. Yet hedonism and distraction do not self-evidently characterize the subjectivity of voluntary work in churches, charities, trade unions and political parties. Nor – to take a less rarefied popular gratification that even Eliot did not overlook – do they account for the forms and practices of sport culture. We need only think of football fans: dauntingly learned, concentrated to the point of obsession, masterful in their urge to second-guess every move in the politics of tournaments and boardrooms, they are a mass-intellectual rebuke to the bimbo-popular. The logical and psychological properties that Chambers assigns to 'contemplation' are necessary conditions of all knowledge, not only the academic kind. In slighting them, he light-mindedly reduces his notion of 'popular epistemology' to self-contradiction. The appeal to the 'tactile' and the 'visceral' seems streetwise, but it is more easily recognized in its normal academic setting, as an irrationalist philosophy of 'life' – or, in literary studies, as dogmatic anti-intellectualism in the style of D.H. Lawrence. Chambers's dualistic scheme of disembodied intellectual contemplation and mindless popular distraction illustrates that recurring tendency in Cultural Studies to invert the basic categories of Kulturkritik, and, in its distinctive individual extremism, projects it into one likely future. An adequate cultural theory would have to find ways of understanding the insistent life of the body in signification of all kinds – the 'contemplative' theoretical tradition of psychoanalysis has been precisely such an attempt. But when, as here, the popular is drained of conceptuality, and then promoted as a model of intellectual practice, there is no longer either theory or culture, and Cultural Studies is left to contemplate its own end.

Chambers championed his popular epistemology in the face of 'culture ... with a capital C' and its typically contemplative interpreter, the academic. Two years later – in 1988, the year of Morris's intervention – Dick Hebdige advanced the cause of 'banality' against another kind of intellectual. Post-dating the first engagement with popular culture to the installation of the first Thatcher government in 1979 – a recollection that seems to mistake autobiography for collective history – Hebdige queried the general political rationale for such departures. Should not popular culture be studied for its own sake, rather than for high-minded political reasons? It is indeed 'banal', but 'vitally', not 'fatally' so. However, this vitality charges the popular-cultural process itself, not the constructed object of analysis, which in reality has served as 'the glass on to which generations of intellectuals have been projecting so many of their own largely unadmitted desires and anxieties'. In this brusque interpretive reduction, Hebdige challenged metacultural discourse as a whole, including his own disciplinary formation and its declared political tasks. The 'aspirations' that animated the giant Live Aid concert of summer 1985 – the event that Stuart Hall took for a movement – were in the end 'more *profound* than the quest of intellectuals either to merge with the imaginary masses or to triumph in their disappearance' (Hebdige 1988).

Here is a vision still bolder than that of Chambers: the reconciliation of subject and object in post-Cultural Studies, the intellectual as fan. It is not easy to discern the position from which Hebdige could now speak. His judgement depended for its authority on precisely the kind of intellectual 'merging' with the people that it rejected as self-deluding. In this it bears a close family resemblance to the old Cretan Paradox, the kind of statement that, if true, is false, and vice versa. It is relevant to note that Hebdige's conclusion echoed, at a range of seventy years, the words of another ironist who defended a self-affirming culture against intellectual schematism, fearing, in all such presumption, 'the end of music'. As Thomas Mann not only might have said, but very nearly did say: 'Banality may be fatal to the intellect. ... On the other hand, it may just save our lives' (Hebdige 1988: 32; and cf. p. 6 above)

ORGANIC INTELLECTUALS?

Chambers and Hebdige bear witness, euphorically in one case, ironically in the other, to the existential project of the Birmingham Centre, which was 'organizational': that is, the formation of a new kind of intellectual, who, in Stuart Hall's parting formulation, would

> aim to become more 'organic' to new and emergent tendencies in society, who [would] seek to become more integral with those forces, linked to them, capable of reflecting what Gramsci called 'the intellectual function' in its wider, non-specialist and non-elitist sense.
>
> (Hall 1980a: 46)

Hall's words are worth repeating now, in the light of a longer retrospect from the early 1990s:

> we were trying to find an institutional practice in cultural studies that might produce an organic intellectual. We didn't know

> previously what that would mean, in the context of Britain in the 1970s, and we weren't sure we would recognize him or her if we managed to produce it. ... [We] couldn't tell then, and can hardly tell now, where that emerging historical movement was to be found. We were organic intellectuals without any organic point of reference; organic intellectuals with a nostalgia or will or hope ... that at some point we would be prepared in intellectual work for that kind of relationship, if such a conjuncture ever appeared. More truthfully, we were prepared to imagine or model or simulate such a relationship in its absence. ... We never connected with that rising movement; it was a metaphoric exercise.
>
> (Hall [1992] 1996e: 267–8)

These sentences relay Hall's abiding sense of difficulty, and his awareness of the 'necessary modesty' of committed intellectual work. But as a reflection on a period, they do not carry conviction. They seem disarming rather than self-critical, and thus attract the closer attention they discourage. Emergent historical movements, familiar, new or reinvented, proliferated in that diversely militant decade. Feminist and black struggles, which Hall singles out only a paragraph later, provoked formative crises throughout British society, as they did in the Centre for Contemporary Cultural Studies. Perhaps the greatest among the myriad problems of the time was that of the emergent tendencies of capital and the right – and here it is proper to remember Hall's early, ambitious analyses of Thatcherism (Hall and Jacques 1983), and to note the 'organic' role of Cultural Studies intellectuals in the last years of British Communism, as expositors of the New Times that also nurtured New Labour (Rustin 1989). Hall's rhetorical emphasis on collective cognitive impotence – what 'we' did not know, were unsure of, might not recognize, and so on – marks an even more curious feature of this desolate retrospect, namely, that it becomes plausible only on the drastic condition

that the available political knowledges of those days are suspended, put under erasure or simply nullified. Such indeed is the
implication of Chambers's 'epistemology', which reduces the very
idea of popular politics to self-contradiction, and of Hebdige's
creative embrace of banality, with its counterpart dismissal of
leftist aspiration as a symptom of intellectual pathology. And in
this, paradoxically, they illustrate a possible version of organicism,
as Hall defined it. Broad, non-specialist, non-elitist intelligence:
or distraction on the town. This is organicism as farce.

Yet Birmingham fostered such developments of thought as
true varieties of its general orientation, whose bearings were not
entirely what they were taken to be. The most striking feature of
Hall's Gramscian vision of organicization is that it effectively displaces Gramsci's own categories. Hall reinvents the classic distinction between 'traditional' and 'organic' intellectuals – which
is crucially historical and social-structural in its sense – as one between academicist and partisan dispositions and styles of practice.
At the same time, he transfers to the second, privileged term, the
'organic', the identifying properties of the first. Gramsci's traditional intellectuals were typically broad and non-specialist in
ethos, and represented themselves as a distinct and cohesive body
serving a general social interest. They could do so because of their
objective character as adaptive residues from older class formations. Organic intellectuals, in contrast, arose from fundamental
social classes and represented them metonymically, as any part
may represent a whole, and not merely in virtue of a free act of
commitment: as the conspicuous biological metaphor implies,
Gramsci understood them as intellectuals *of* and *for* their social
group, a specialized function of its general historical life-process
(Gramsci 1971: 5–14). In Hall's reading, however, social–
structural determinations dissolve into a pattern of more or less
conscious, resolute 'alignments', and organic intellectuals assume
the moralized form of a partisan popular tendency within the
field of the traditional (Hall [1986] 1996b: 433). The matter at

issue here is not scriptural. On the contrary, an adequate, purposeful discussion of the problematics of 'organicism' – which is indeed crucial for any project of social transformation – would entail uninhibited critical development beyond Gramsci. What counts for now is the discursive ambiguity of the organicizing motif in Birmingham Cultural Studies. The characteristic of traditional intelligentsias, as Gramsci understood them, cannot be reduced to everyday academic practice – with which it is then possible, against discouraging odds, to make a politically committed break. The tradition of unspecialized intelligence, in its sublimated form as stewardship of the general social interest, has always presupposed a break of a rather different kind – as the prophets of European Kulturkritik, traditional intellectuals par excellence, all confirm. The very idea of a political break is uncomprehending, in a domain – that of culture – whose imputed truth is a critique of all politics, of politics as such.[4]

THE 'POLITICS' OF METACULTURE

The thought seems incongruous. Stuart Hall has maintained that, however much Cultural Studies may vary, as it invents or reinvents itself in new locations, its constitutive interest must lie in the nexus of representations and 'power' (1997: 30). Martin Barker and Anne Beezer are among those who resist what they perceive as a 'new paradigm' that displaces 'power as a central concept', while retaining their belief in a disciplinary subject, 'we', that would reassert that centrality (1991: 9). Richard Johnson, Hall's successor at CCCS, has characterized the Birmingham intervention as a 'struggle to reform the "old left" politics', as 'a constructive quarrel with dominant styles within the Labor Movement, especially the neglect of cultural conditions of politics, and a mechanical narrowing of politics itself' (Johnson 1996: 79). 'We' are nothing if not 'political'.

Johnson's formulation is admirable as a synopsis of early New

Left intellectual strategy; it remains contemporary, and would probably win wide assent in his discipline. Whether it accurately describes the stronger tendency in Cultural Studies practice is nevertheless debatable. Here is David Morley, taking issue with 'the relativist, self-reflexive orthodoxy' now installed in his field:

> the overall effect of much of this has in the end been a disabling one, as a result of which it becomes pretty hard for anyone to say anything about anyone (or anything) else, for fear of accusation of ontological imperialism. Apart from other considerations, and despite the declared political credentials (and intentions) of much of this kind of work, within cultural studies, this is in fact, politically disabling. It is hard to mobilize around a political platform of principled uncertainty, especially if one of those principles is that it is ultimately impossible to know what is going on.
>
> (Morley 1997: 122)

And here is Angela McRobbie, looking back on her influential study of the girls weekly *Jackie*, which she has come to fault as inadequate in its appreciation of such practices as day-dreaming at work:

> to ignore these more private aspects of everyday experience is to avoid considering their function and how they make sense in terms of politics and social change.
>
> (cited in McGuigan 1992: 110)

Next, Lawrence Grossberg, on 'the current roadblock in cultural studies':

> its inability to address the specificity of the relations between popular culture and systemic politics in the context of a hegemonic struggle.
>
> (cited in McGuigan 1992: 214)

Finally, then, Iain Chambers, distilling the critical insight of his *Popular Culture*:

> It is an argument about popular aesthetics, about disposable
> culture, about everyday perception and ultimately about the
> sense, the politics of our world.
>
> (Chambers 1986: 190)

Here, cumulatively, is the Cultural Studies imagination. Morley, McRobbie and Grossberg offer the same narrative of realization, tracing in the curve of a paragraph or even a sentence the passage from philosophy, day-dreams or disciplinary agendas to platforms, struggle and social change. In Chambers, the narrative is already complete: as the syntactic parallelism suggests, his list is not a sequence of topics but a set of equivalences. There may be, as Todd Gitlin has judged, a 'consolatory' logic at work in this imagination – the reflex of a left-wing generation making its way in the great reactionary tides of the late twentieth century. Perhaps it distinguishes a phase in a long history of what Stuart Hall has termed 'politics by other means' – specifically, an alternative means of furthering the early ambition of the British New Left (1990). Or perhaps – this further thought does not cancel the others – an older, more basic desire has renewed its pressure.

Politics is everywhere in Cultural Studies. The word appears on nearly every page of the corpus. Only 'culture' itself has greater salience in the general discourse of the subject. Truly commonplace in this respect, yet also predictably urgent in its stress, 'politics' functions in this quarter as an expletive. It is, in pragmatic effect, the *p*-word. Expletives are propositionally redundant; their discursive function is, as linguists say, 'phatic', determining the conditions of a communicative exchange rather than its paraphrasable conceptual content. The *p*-word in Cultural Studies is predominantly phatic in accent, confirming a relationship, an identity and, implicitly, a desire. That desire is not merely to remain politically committed in the face of institutionalizing pressures, and not even only to help cultivate a more adequate political imagination in the left; it is, in Gitlin's further, more disturbing critical judgement, simply 'to *be* politics' (1997: 37).

What might it mean to 'claim to *be* politics'? Johnson's critical stress on the 'cultural conditions of politics', which follows as a necessary and weighty consequence of the theoretical mutation that led to Cultural Studies, precludes such a claim, implying as it does the non-identity of cultural and politics, and a knowing subject irreducible to either. In the discursive formation from which he was speaking, however, the strategic meaning of the culture/politics distinction was quite specific. The 'cultural conditions' were the typical preferences of the social majority – popular culture – and the politics that of the organized left, and to each there corresponded a kind of intellectual: the organic to whose function Birmingham aspired, and the traditional, the ideologues of what might be called politics with a capital P. So configured, the 'constructive quarrel' assumed a form that belied the apparent sense of the distinction, becoming, in practice, a struggle to establish the sovereignty of culture over politics in the disputed territory of the popular. In this, for Cultural Studies, lay the meaning of the New Times venture, which really did enact a 'claim to *be* politics' in the most drastic metaphoric sense of an old saying: 'we are what we eat'. The manifest rationale of that venture – a defining moment in the life of the British Cultural Studies intelligentsia – was to refashion the sensibility of a dullard left. Its objective discursive impulse was to subsume the political under the cultural, to undo the rationality of politics as a determinate social form. It is time to recall that Leavis and *Scrutiny* also urged constructive engagement with the cultural conditions of politics, in a critical practice whose logic belied the relative modesty of its claims. Kulturkritik reasoned politics out of moral existence, as a false pretender to authority. Cultural Studies, inverting the social commitments of that tradition but retaining its discursive form, has been tempted to follow suit. And to the extent that it has yielded, it has disclosed its character as a strictly limited mode of opposition to Kulturkritik, with which it continues to share the discursive space of metaculture.

PART III

METACULTURE AND SOCIETY

The record of European Kulturkritik in the twentieth century bears witness to its force: its power of attraction as a way of evaluating modernity, and – no less impressive – its ability to absorb radical challenges to its presumptive truth. The cultural studies tradition took shape in radical opposition to Kulturkritik, but my critical claim has been that there too metacultural discourse has remained tendentially dominant. That is, it has not simply been the dominant tendency, but the discourse that spontaneously tends to dominate. Such an assertion is inevitably controversial. Actually existing Cultural Studies is a heterogeneous formation. Intellectual purity has never been seen as a rule to observe or a goal to attain in its strategies of self-development, and the pragmatic conditions of late-century academic existence have in fact tended to favour rather than frustrate this preference. (The discipline is better adapted to its environment than its devotees or their traditionalist detractors like to think.) Yet throughout this impure formation there runs a critical differential, a theme that marks off the idea of Cultural Studies proper from the various theories and methods that support the teaching and research programmes carried on in its name. What has distinguished this project–discipline from the ordinary run of theories and sociologies of culture is its impulse to create its analytic object as a subject: to establish what is spoken of as the entity that speaks of it. Thus, it seeks to validate a new cultural subject, and, in final effect, to institute culture as the authoritative subject of a discourse on social relations.

Culture, here, is more than a corpus of forms and practices, however radically extended in range. It is more even than the social whole seen in its signifying aspect: as in Kulturkritik, it is the principle, the condition of valid social judgement. Benda's eternal truths, Mann's nation and Leavis's human values were variant embodiments of this indivisible authority, in the name of which they uttered their critiques of modern social particularism, and, above all, of those interests they associated with 'mass' existence. Cultural Studies has displaced the notion of the mass for the sake of the subaltern popular, and therewith discomposed the authoritative subject of Kultur in the interest of a radical alternative. But in doing so much yet no more, it has reproduced the discursive form of what it seeks to overcome. The stake is not the scope of what is held to be 'culture', or the pattern of social values inscribed in it – as if the old Kulturkritik were at fault only in its narrowness and traditionalism. What is at issue here is that principle. It is the *status* of the cultural, and specifically its relation to the established form of general social authority, namely politics. Kulturkritik did not doubt its entitlements: politics is inherently deficient as a mode of general authority, which can emerge only from the elusive life of the whole, or culture. Cultural Studies could scarcely recognize itself in such terms, but nevertheless so it has spoken, constituting itself as a permanent rebuke to the upstart authorities of 'the left'. If the *p*-word in Cultural Studies discourse often seems as empty as it is insistent, this is because the desire that powers it is, in the context, unspeakable. Culture, now popular and oppositional, and represented by the 'organic intellectuals' of the new project–discipline, takes over the prerogatives once vested in another kind of intellectual. Metacultural discourse is metapolitics, the be all and end all of (left) political reason.

THE DESIRE CALLED CULTURAL STUDIES

How might this uncanny phenomenon be accounted for?[1] Cultural Studies has become a part of its own corpus in recent years, as commentators explore the logic of its emergence and tendencies of development, laying special emphasis on its immediate social and political contexts. Jim McGuigan notes its specific appeal for those without secure social antecedents for their identity as intellectuals – first-generation working-class graduates, and 'in general for those from positions of social subordination and marginality' (1992: 11–12). He also notes the formative pressure of a more concentrated sectoral interest, a new 'class fraction', neither bourgeois nor intellectual in anterior senses, but implanted now in culturally central practices of 'presentation and representation' – the media and the publicity industry. Out of this determinate historical configuration, he suggests, comes 'the populist intervention in cultural knowledge' that is Cultural Studies, and which 'can be understood, in the first instance, as a ... struggle for symbolic power, representing fairly narrow interests yet similarly evincing a certain democratization of culture: a postmodern populism' (p. 220). Uncritical populism thus appears as an inborn behavioural propensity, in which 'solidarity' tends to degenerate into 'sentimentality', which is in effect a kind of social conformism. John Fiske's notions of semiotic democracy, of television as a liberated cultural zone, are 'homologous' with the neoliberal dogma of consumer choice, McGuigan observes. They are a mock-oppositional replay of the leading ideology in contemporary capitalism.

This sociological hypothesis coexists with a critical judgement of uncertain explanatory status, concerning, as it happens, the fading of explanation as an intellectual value in Cultural Studies. McGuigan condemns the growing preference for sympathetic interpretation as a priority in the analysis of popular consumption, and the corresponding want of attention to structural conditions of cultural practices, and calls for a reunification of interpretive and explanatory forms of inquiry. But, beyond this, he is also tempted to consider this partitioning of theory and method as a causal factor in the growth of 'uncritical populism'. Todd Gitlin, on the other hand, although writing in a spirit akin to McGuigan's, sees in the narrative of Cultural Studies the imprint of a specifically political history. Gitlin endorses the formative ambitions of Cultural Studies in its own customary terms. He seconds early New Left perceptions of the increasing social weight of popular culture in post-war capitalism, and of the unfamiliar, perhaps politically significant collective subjectivities taking form within it. But he is correspondingly astringent in his assessment of the new project–discipline as it evolved in the political conjunctures of the 1970s and 1980s. Cultural Studies, he writes,

> is a form of intellectual life that answers to passions and hopes imported into its precincts from outside. Cultural studies may not be a significant social movement beyond the precincts of certain academies [Gitlin is alluding here to a characteristically grandiose claim on behalf of the discipline], but it certainly responds to the energies of social and cultural movements – and their eclipse.
>
> (Gitlin 1997: 25–6)

Gitlin's thesis is that the political claims of Cultural Studies have developed in inverse proportion to the actual political fortunes of the wider left of which it has been a part. It has fashioned itself as a redemptive substitute for blocked or defeated movements:

> Perhaps it was youth culture that would inaugurate, cement,

ennoble the rising class that inevitably would displace and overcome the ruling groups! At least popular culture had vitality, rebelliousness, oppositional spirit – and then, by implication, so could the people who made it popular. If political power was foreclosed, the battlements of culture still remained to be taken! Or perhaps – if one really believed that the personal was political – they had already been taken. Or perhaps the only reason politics looked unavailing was that the wrong culture was in force.

(1997: 29)

More sympathetic, for all his broad parody, than McGuigan, Gitlin is equally severe in his judgement on Cultural Studies conformism, and not at all academicist in his sense of the necessary corrective:

[Is] there a chance of a modest redemption? Perhaps, if we imagine a harder-headed, less wishful cultural studies, free of the burden of imagining itself to be a political practice. A chastened, realistic cultural studies would divest itself of political pretensions. It would not claim to *be* politics. ... It would be less romantic about the world but also about itself. Less would be more.

(1997: 37)

The *p*-word, no longer compulsively uttered, might recover some of its critical force.

BETWEEN PAST AND FUTURE

McGuigan's sociological conjecture and Gitlin's political reading furnish important elements of an understanding of Cultural Studies. In themselves, however, they lack both specificity and generality. A fully concrete account would have to be strictly comparative, neither assuming the world-defining significance of the British experience nor reducing the ambiguities of its singular international effectivity. At the same time – and this is the crucial consideration in this setting of argument – it would not mistake local specificity for uniqueness in time and space. It would not defer to the assumption – which is that of Cultural Studies itself – that the discursive formation to be explained is a novelty, or only a novelty, a recent creation of distinctively recent conditions. Gitlin accepts this assumption, if only by default, with the interesting result that his perceptions exceed the terms of his explanation. The specificities of the 1970s cannot have given rise to a phenomenon that long predates them. The cultural impulse 'to *be* politics' is older and more general. 'The anti-political populism of Cultural Studies', as Gitlin terms it, seems less a development, be it for good or for ill, than a case of persistence, if not regressive fixation, a paradoxical episode in the history of metaculture. It is this discursive formation, not the record of Cultural Studies, which is only one of its sites of elaboration, that is centrally in question here.

'The working-out of the idea of culture', Raymond Williams once wrote, 'is a slow reach again for control' (1961: 285). The placing of *control*, at the close of a sentence and also a paragraph, in the concluding chapter of *Culture and Society*, marks its critical importance. There is more to say about this (though it is worth noting at once that in English, compared with other languages sharing the Latin original, the word can be ambiguous, semantically associated not merely with *checking* or *monitoring* but also with the far stronger meanings of *dominance* or *command*). But first, however, we should pause to consider the temporality here inscribed in 'the idea of culture'. The 'working-out' and the 'slow reach' imply a progressive movement towards a point of transcendence, in which a persisting condition – the reach is slow – is negated. But into the phrasing of this temporality Williams inserts the stylistically awkward *again*, thus invoking a second, distinct temporality in which the future becomes the moment of recovery, the making good not merely of lack but of loss. The functioning of these distinct temporalities in metacultural discourse is complex in the strict sense: neither is the inner truth of the other, and they vary to extremes, from case to case, in their relative force. It is the more interesting, then, that Williams, who knew this, should nevertheless have emphasized their joint implication in a single historical practice.

Intuitions of loss define the temporal imagination of Kulturkritik. Be it of a whole national mentality (Mann) or of a rarefied spiritual discipline (Benda), of political or cultural order (Ortega, Leavis) or of a cohesive social scheme of perception and interest (Mannheim), the loss is always one of integral authority. The past is the standard from which modernity has erred, and the pattern – if there is one – of adjustment. For Mann and Benda, the only strategic options were personal, the ethical disciplines of irony or contemplation. Ortega turned to prophecy. Leavis and Mannheim canvassed activist solutions in the public sphere. All substantiated their claims to critical integrity in imageries of aristocracy or priesthood, the historic types of a general authority they would honour as recusants in exile or, deceptively, as a new meritocracy in the face of the modern iconoclasts. Mannheim and Leavis coupled the temporalities of transcendence and recovery in efficient schemes of cultural substitution, in which new educational elites would recover something of the authority of old hierarchies. (Eliot, the settled reactionary, perceived as much, and stiffened his defences accordingly: Kultur was not, in truth, best served by Kritik, which might educate a Cromwell – or, at any rate, a Hoggart.) For another pair, Woolf and Orwell, no such discursive finesse was available. They wrote in solidarity with subaltern social interests – those of women and workers, respectively – that could not easily be sublimated into an ideal community of the mind, a location that neither of them was, in any case, pre-adapted to occupy. The double temporality of 'culture'

worked here, too, producing visions of emancipation but also a
damaging ambivalence. Woolf drew on the literary past for her
image of an androgynous future, but was also drawn back to it, as
a time before the onset of feminist agitation and a crisis-ridden
'sex consciousness'.[2] Orwell called for a socialist revolution powered by a national–popular England – which was, however, the
spiritual base from which he launched his own rhetorical insur-
rections against his fellow intellectuals of the left.

The later tradition of metaculture has dispensed with all such
temporal couplings, efficient or not. If Eliot, in his conservatism,
exemplified the flat rejection of social transcendence, seeking
only to confirm inherited cultural inequality, his true antithesis is
Cultural Studies, which incarnates the will to negation, in the interests of emancipatory change. *No longer...* is the time signal of
the discipline. The past is that which must (now) be repudiated,
be it Kulturkritik or a certain Marxist economism, which in this
discourse appear as strict complements, both figuring the annulment of popular creativity. Or – for the axiom is reversible – that
which is to be repudiated must for that very reason be rendered as
past, even at the cost of apparent self-contradiction: the temporal-
izing rhetoric of Stuart Hall's commentary on New Times is an
epitome of this (pp. 117ff. above). The typical Cultural Studies
subject – the practitioner as advocate of the disciplinary project –
itself enacts this compulsive modernism, always announcing itself
as if for the first time, shedding what it would otherwise have to
assume as a formative, therefore limiting, history, a past of one's
own. At a comfortable extreme – which, as the cases of Iain
Chambers and Dick Hebdige illustrate, is not merely hypotheti-
cal – this modernism is indeed objectively conformist. A certain
kind of organic intellectual reverses Eliot's traditionalism and
lives the present as though it were the desirable future – which,
once it has been conjured into actuality in this way ceases to exist
as a critical force capable of passing judgement on what actually
exists. However, to insist one-sidedly on the banalizing effect of

such gestures would itself be an act of banalization. Metacultural discourse in the left-modernist variation that is Cultural Studies incarnates the impulse to accelerate Williams's slow reach for control, a utopian desire to be – actually *be* – one step ahead of its own validating historical process.

METACULTURE AND SOCIETY

The motifs of 'acceleration' and measured anticipation (a practice '*one* step ahead' of its own process) come from the days of Thomas Mann's *Reflections*. Their source is a lecture given by the Marxist critic and philosopher Georg Lukács in June 1919, in his capacity as a Commissar for Education and Culture in the Hungarian revolutionary government.[3] The urgent purpose of the lecture, 'The Changing Function of Historical Materialism', was to define the specificity of socialist revolution and, in particular, to vindicate the role of 'violence', the moment of deliberate force in political practice, in its making. However, as the title suggests, Lukács built his case from arguments of the most general kind, which, it will quickly emerge, go to the heart of the question of metacultural discourse.[4] His fundamental theoretical intent was a critique of 'economics'. The historical achievement of capitalism, and its difference as a system from all its predecessors, he maintained, lay in its unprecedented power to transform the given material world, to transcend 'natural limits' (Lukács 1971: 233). Yet in the same measure, the specifically social relations and objectives that would henceforward be historically dominant themselves assumed the special, apparently natural form of 'economics', a social form in which the realities so designated appeared, along with law and the state, as a '*closed*' system, an apparatus 'apparently quite independent, hermetic and autonomous' (p. 230). Marx had classically criticized the 'vulgar' economists who abstracted the capitalist market from its constitutive social relations and eternalized it as economic nature. Now, Lukács argued, vulgar Marxism had done likewise, mistaking the specifically capitalist form of economic life for an anthropological constant, a 'law' of history. The laws of economic nature, be that eternal or evolutionary, were indices of alienated social relations. In cancelling the reality, revolution would also 'annul' the law. The moment of 'socialization', Lukács declared, entails a restructuring of property relations but also, and in consequence of that, a transformation of the status of 'the economic' within the social whole. It involves *a turning in the direction of something qualitatively new*, that is, 'conscious action directed towards the comprehended totality of society' (p. 250). Violence – or mass revolutionary politics – breaks 'the hold of reified relations over man and the hold of economics over society', and clears the approach to a state of things in which 'ideology' becomes the dominant, 'the authentic content of human life' (pp. 251–2).

If Lukács's prospectus seems to us to evince a richly period quality, that is a reflection on our own historical parochialism. The problem he tackled here is that of metaculture itself. The theme of 'economics' will be familiar to any reader of Raymond Williams and Stuart Hall as that of 'base and superstructure' – indeed Williams, in an independent parallel development of thought, constructed his own critique in the same substantive terms (pp. 83–92 above).[5] However, with greater lucidity than either, Lukács associated the theoretical crux of economic determinism with the politico-cultural crux of deliberative authority (the idea of 'a consciously directed society' [1971: 251]), and proposed an integrated solution to them. Economic determinism is not so much pure error, Lukács argued in effect, as a false generalization from the historically distinctive reality of capitalism, which constitutes 'the economic' as a specialized, autonomous process and favours corresponding forms of social reason – 'economics'. The necessary corollaries for a society thus governed by 'economic compulsion' are an instrumentalized politics (a form of governance based on submission to an intractable real world) and an ineffectual culture (valued but useless 'principles that [can] occur only as "superstructure"', as secondary, dependent). In other words, a structurally induced enfeeblement of authority and power of social deliberation. In this, too, capitalism differs constitutionally from preceding and succeeding forms of society. Although Lukács did not say so much, it is consistent with his analysis to recall the fatalistic discourses of social authority – religious or traditionalist – that transfigured the 'natural limits' of feudalism. He was of course emphatic in his conviction that socialism could outstrip not only 'natural limits' but those of 'economics and violence' as well, creating the conditions of a politics consisting in what had 'until now' been 'merely "Ideology"' – or culture.

The historical context of Lukács's argument was socialist revolution, achieved (in Russia) or in progress (in his native Hungary and elsewhere in Central Europe). It is capitalism that must concern us here. Lukács's basic claim, in its first, Marxian form, is that the capitalist mode of production is necessarily anarchic, in the strongest sense: it is finally ungovernable (Marx [1869] 1976: 635, 667). Yet the epoch of capitalism has also been that of politics, the locus and means of the struggle for social self-determination according to one or another available formulation of that distinctively modern end: liberty, democracy, independence, equality, welfare, socialism. Bourgeois civilization has exalted politics in socio-economic conditions that sooner or later thwart all but the best-adapted of programmes. This historic paradox, which has intensified over the decades since Lukács wrote, with the widening of popular claims to entitlement and participation in public affairs, has done more than any local disappointment or scandal, however great in itself, to discredit the very idea of politics. But if politics as deliberative intervention in social relations as a whole is the supreme instance of 'general labour', it is not the only one. Culture, after all, is coextensive with social relations as a whole – and can, indeed, be represented, in specific cultural practices, such as that of Kulturkritik, as an alternative community of meanings and values. For Herbert Marcuse, writing in the heroic phase of twentieth-century Kulturkritik, the modern ideal of culture functioned as a contemplative resolution of the objective disorder of bourgeois society. Raymond Williams's *Culture and Society*, which, for all its differences of style and procedure, offers a congruent interpretation, traced the formation of culture as 'an abstraction and an absolute', as the last court of appeal.[6] Matthew Arnold, who was the pivotal figure in Williams's history, looked towards an ideal fusion of culture in that sense with its practical equivalent, the state. Metacultural discourse has been the form in which culture dissolves the political and takes up the general labour proper to it, assuming the role of a valid social authority.

However, the terms and agencies of that authority are not simply given. Culture, precisely because it is no less but also no more than the instance of meaning in social relations, is wholly implicated in all social antagonism, and, latterly, as 'the culture industry', in the ordinary conflicts of capitalist production itself. Intelligentsias, diverse in their provenance, occupational composition and social affinities, do not spontaneously give voice to a self-evident general interest. Even more so than politics, therefore, culture and intellectuals alike appear both central and marginal, commanding and merely pretentious, sublime and ridiculous, everything and nothing. Paul Valéry's satiric dream-vision has lost none of its sting:

> Tatters of dream came to me. I formed figures which I called 'Intellectuals'. Men almost motionless, who caused great movement in the world. Or very animated men, by the lively action of whose hands and mouths, imperceptible powers and essentially invisible objects were made manifest. ... Men of *thought*, Men of *letters*, Men of *science*, Artists – Causes, living causes, individuate causes, minimal causes, causes within

causes and inexplicable to themselves – and causes whose effects were as vain, but at the same time as prodigiously important, *as I wished.* ... The universe of these causes and their effects existed and did not exist. This system of strange acts, productions, and prodigies had the all-powerful and vacant reality of a game of cards. Inspirations, meditations, works, glory, talents, it took no more than a certain look to make these things nearly everything, and a certain other look to reduce them to nearly nothing. ... [And among these intellectuals] the most ridiculous were those who made themselves, on their own authority, the judges and justices of the tribe.

(Valéry 1948: 61–2)

Such images of culture and intellectuals are stock items in everyday discourse, polite and popular, and with good historical cause. What Marx said of the quarrel between romantics and utilitarians applies equally to the vexatious problems of 'culture' and 'intellectuals': they are commonplaces in the spontaneous discourse of capitalist society, and will go on circulating 'up to its blessed end' (Marx 1973: 162). Seeking always to manage the objective social contradictions that irritate it into life, metacultural discourse is constitutionally dependent on a rhetoric of 'splitting'. In a process akin to that described in the psychoanalytic tradition, the ambivalences and ambiguities of 'culture' and 'intellectuals' in a capitalist society are rewritten as fateful polarities of good and bad, true and false, high and low.[7] Kulturkritik offers the simpler illustration: 'culture' (good) must repeatedly discover 'civilization' (bad) and its approaching catastrophe, which is what confirms its own identity and mission. Intellectuals must either conform to their moral essence or pervert it. They are either true *clercs* or treacherous accomplices of the market and the masses. Cultural Studies, a complex formation in which metacultural discourse is tendentially dominant but not necessarily so, presents a more variegated picture, but not a fundamentally different one.

Would-be organic intellectuals, who may go so far as to renounce the title of intellectual for the common world of fans, must repeatedly discover the truth of popular culture, must always bear witness to it in defiance of the powers of 'culture with a capital C', which is also the left with a capital 'L'.

Metacultural discourse, it might be said, is a form of resistance through ritual, offering what the Birmingham circle would once have conceptualized as a 'magical solution' to the poverty of politics in bourgeois society. The difference between its older and more recent phases is one of temporality. Seen as Lukács saw it, the perverse autonomy of 'economics' in the capitalist mode of production is uncheckable. 'Conscious action directed towards the comprehended totality of society' is inconceivable except as revolution. 'Socialization' of production, its 'annulment' in the reified form of 'economics', is the structural condition of a collective life in which culture might really become the social dominant. And that outcome is contingent upon the mustering and exercise of effective political force in and against the historical present. Metacultural discourse elaborates the alternative, which itself assumes two forms. Kulturkritik looks to the past for the symbolic metapolitical forces capable of subduing civilized anarchy. *Scrutiny*'s images of public virtue, of 'disinterested' governance of the whole, were feudal in provenance. Its critical meritocrats, like Mannheim's, would be a new priesthood. In Cultural Studies, the unquenched desire for an emancipated future has powered a symbolic transformation of the present. In the great commodity display of modern times, where Kulturkritik saw only indifference, standardization and levelling down, Cultural Studies prefers to see only use-values, sensuousness and a rainbow of discretionary potential. The fascination with 'youth' is telling. The slow reach has attained the speed of time travel. It can seem, on a good day, as if Lukács's vision has been realized, as if popular culture has outrun 'mere ideology' and the 'violence' of politics, to take final, unmediated possession of itself and its social world.

The authority that metacultural discourse recalls from the past promotes order and wholeness. The authority it alternatively borrows from the future affirms difference – and that not only as diversity, but as the heterogeneity that asserts itself within the normalizing frames of reason or humanity or nation, disrupting them. That contrast is historically substantial, as any comparative biographical survey of Kulturkritik and Cultural Studies would show. Yet, it has not been sufficient to rupture the formal continuity of metaculture, which, in either mode, invents an authoritative subject, 'good' culture, be it minority or popular, whose function is to mediate a symbolic metapolitical resolution of the contradictions of capitalist modernity. Popular culture, as it appears in this rarefied discursive construction, replays the dialectic of the high tradition that concerned Marcuse in the 1930s: it, too is 'affirmative', in both the good and the bad senses. The excitable 'conformism' and 'populism' for which Cultural Studies has been chided run parallel to the negativism and elitism of Kulturkritik. They, too, are driven by an ambiguous 'promise of happiness'. Conformity here is not merely pragmatic adaptation to an overwhelming reality, even if it must always resemble that, but a deflated utopianism.

CULTURAL POLITICS?

Metacultural discourse is a creature of discrepancy, for which it constitutes itself as resolution. The discrepancy is that of culture and politics in the plane of social authority. In the earlier phase, that of Kulturkritik, the critique of politics is flat and final. Politics cannot metabolize the moral insights of culture, and is therefore inherently deficient as a social form. If not shunned altogether, as Benda preferred, it must be regulated by a superordinate politics of mind. Cultural Studies repudiates this tradition on demonstratively political grounds, but only to submit 'its own' polity, that of the left, to the same critique,

with comparable effects. The progressive foregrounding of subjectivity in Cultural Studies, and the privileging of identity as
the site and stake of social antagonism, achieve far more than
the enrichment and complication they plausibly offer – or
rather, much less than that – if, in theoretical reality, there is
no longer a valid and specifically political practice to enrich or
complicate. The problem that animates and seemingly justifies
metacultural discourse, is not, at bottom, one of moral substance – having to do with specific social interests and purposes – however graphically the 'content' of politics may have
featured in the record of critical controversy. It is one of form.

Only the typical dualism of Kulturkritik – the splitting of
culture and civilization – obscures the insight on which Cultural
Studies is founded. If culture, in its general reality, is the moment
of meaning in social relations, if it is nothing less but also nothing more than the sense-making element of all practice, then it
cannot also be exalted as the higher moral tribunal before which
the lower claims of politics must submit to arbitration. On the
contrary, and for the same reason, there is no instance of culture
that is exempt from political implication. But the same sanction
must then apply to popular culture, which, likewise, may not be
privileged as Cultural Studies would wish. Moreover, to pass from
that crucial founding insight to the commonplace that 'everything is political' is to scant the apparently contradictory insight
on which Kulturkritik drew for its compelling pejorative visions
of modernity: politics is never everything. This seems paradoxical. After all, the specific practice of politics is to determine the
totality of social relations in a given space. But this quintessen-
tially general labour is specialized in mode. It is normally deliberative in character, governed by the question, What is to be
done? Political utterance, then, is always injunctive, regardless of
its medium, occasion or genre. It wills, urges, dictates. Its aim is
to secure assent (a process in which issues of identity are indeed
central) and, failing that, compliance, of which coercion furnishes

the last guarantee. Cultural practices proper – those second-order elaborations of social meaning whose principal function is signification – have no need of that modal specialization, or no authoritative access to it, even where they pursue 'political' ends. They lack the formal distinction of political practice, from which they differ, correspondingly, in their norms of judgement. Culture may absolutize any value (including, as metaculture, that of itself). It may offer an infinity of moral discriminations, in mutually irreducible patterns. No meaning or value simply translates any other. Politics, whose rationale is to secure this or that general condition of existence, in a determinate social perspective, must always seek optimal terms of alignment, of solidarity and antagonism. Contrariwise, a political project may entail promoting division in a domain of cultural affinity, and for the same basic reason. Thus, as Gramsci perceived (1985: 99–102), political and cultural evaluation tend spontaneously towards non-co-ordination: each with respect to the other is both excessive (too broad, too narrow) and insufficient (too broad, too narrow). The culture-politics discrepancy is always historically specific. It is the crisis of national tradition, or democratic legitimacy, or public standards, or class-consciousness, or ethnic continuity. Nevertheless, discrepancy itself is the general rule.

The rule is general, and also without discernible limit of jurisdiction, for if politics remains modally specialized even when conducted wholly in the plane of culture, then Lukács's vision of free and fluent human self-elaboration must be qualified. Even if cultural practice were to be released from 'mere ideology' and political practice from the necessity of 'violence', the discrepancy would persist into a future beyond lucid imagining. For just so long, Marcuse's 'affirmative culture' would continue in its equivocal elaboration of the promise of happiness, in a purely 'inward' cancellation of objective social contradictions, which would thereby be spared more consequential political attack. And so also, therefore, would metacultural discourse, which is the most general form of that affirmation, synoptic and engaged, embodying the will to resolution. Yet it does not follow necessarily that metaculture constitutes the inescapable discursive condition of critical thought, either in that elusive future or in the more tangible one we already inhabit. The only necessity in the case is that of discrepancy itself, which, once grasped as such, appears in another aspect, not as a place of historic frustration and wish-fulfilment but as a space of possibility.

'Cultural politics' is a spacious category. Socially committed art practice and criticism are a familiar instance. Stuart Hall's explorations of new ethnicities and black popular culture exemplify this kind of cultural politics. Public policy is the ground of another kind, which controversies over national 'heritage' richly illustrate (Wright 1985; Samuel 1994); and in a development especially associated with Tony Bennett, this has assumed the form of 'cultural policy studies' (Bennett 1992).[8] Bennett's project is avowedly reformist, entailing a break from 'criticism' in favour of 'technical' intervention in institutions: 'cultural studies might envisage its role as consisting of the training of cultural technicians' (Bennett 1993: 83). Glenn Jordan and Chris Weedon, in contrast, reaffirm the liberationist mission of the discipline. 'Cultural politics', they say, in their book of that name, 'is the struggle to fix meanings in the interest of particular groups' (Jordan and Weedon 1995: 544):

> Whose culture shall be the official one and whose shall be subordinated? What cultures shall be regarded as worthy of display and which shall be hidden? Whose history shall be remembered and whose marginalized? What images of social life shall be projected and which shall be marginalized? What voices shall be heard and on what basis? This is the realm of cultural politics.
>
> (Jordan and Weedon 1995: 4, typography modified)

These questions are unarguably fundamental. But there is a further question, not itself political, to put in return: is there any cultural practice that would not be politics, or any politics that would not be cultural? It seems not: '*everything* in social and cultural life is fundamentally to do with *power*. It is integral to culture. *All signifying practices – that is, all practices that have meaning – involve relations of power*' (p. 11). The claim lodged here is more emphatic than precise, but its driving impulse seems unmistakable. 'Cultural politics', in a word, to which Jordan and Weedon resort more than once, is 'everything'. Their title is one word too long: the distinction between culture and politics, on which their linkage logically depends, has been talked out of theoretical existence.

This need not happen. In the present context of argument, the idea of cultural politics acquires a precise conceptual value as a critical check on the metacultural dominant, and as the logical ground, though certainly not the substance, of an alternative. It has to be said again, with emphasis, that the analysis I propose here is formal in character, neither implying nor excluding any particular identification in the field of antagonistic social interests – though, as I hope the analysis of metacultural discourse has helped to show, form is not a secondary matter. Cultural politics, as understood here, is not a special case of either politics or culture. Its field of action is mapped in the discrepancy between its constitutive terms, from which also it absorbs the tension that motivates it. Stuart Hall speaks too starkly, and perhaps with a certain romantic prejudice, in defining culture as 'infinite semiosis', sense-making without end, and politics as its equally abstract regulator, 'arbitrary closure' (Hall 1997: 30). Historical formations of culture, as structured social processes, are not so mercurial in their movement as either phrase suggests, and that definition of politics is already culturalist. Nevertheless, he exaggerates to the point. No politics, in so far as it respects its constitutive function, which is to determine the order of social relations as a whole, can adequately replicate the contours and textures of the cultural formation in which it seeks to have effect. The field of identities, interests and values is always excessive. This excess has been simplified and spiritualized as the higher truth of humanity or the nation (Kulturkritik), and then simplified and politicized as the unregarded democracy of everyday life (Cultural Studies), but these alternative versions of the cultural principle are gambits in a space that does not answer to their reductive definitions. The excess has no fixed composition or tendency. It is a heterogeneous mass of possibilities old and new and never mutually translatable, possibilities no longer or not yet and perhaps never to be chartered as bearing general authority, as proper norms of political judgement. Culture is everything, in the sense that there is no social life outside formations of meaning, but it never adds up. Political practice seeks to determine social relations as a whole – a whole more richly differentiated than the subtlest of programmes, which, therefore, can never lucidly aspire to be everything. And in that necessary non-identity lies the very possibility of the activities, the interests, the perspectives that can meaningfully be distinguished as cultural politics.

Stuart Hall has emphasized the 'necessary modesty' of Cultural Studies. The point of these closing pages on the concept of cultural politics is to suggest that the immodesty his project–discipline has learnt willy-nilly from its authoritarian forebear, Kulturkritik, is, in theory at least, not necessary. Genealogy is not destiny. The social desire that metaculture encodes is inextinguishable: what compels it is Herder's 'image of happiness'. But metaculture as a discursive form is romance, a journey through the waste land in search of lost virtue or into an enchanted forest of commodities, where even the future is in season all year round. It is better, surely, to settle for lucidity – to honour the image of happiness 'negatively', as Adorno put it, by retaining the contradictions 'pure and uncompromised' (1981:32) – and to enter cultural politics with a greater modesty that in fact subserves a greater ambition, as the art of the possible.

NOTES

INTRODUCTION

1   For an illuminating discussion, see Lloyd and Thomas 1998.
2   Dover Wilson's scholarly 1932 edition of Arnold's *Culture and Anarchy* (1869) was the first of its kind; the journal *Scrutiny*, which was launched in Cambridge in the same year, 1932, pursued an avowedly Arnoldian cultural strategy; the USA's leading Arnoldian, Lionel Trilling, published his biography, *Matthew Arnold* (New York: W.W. Norton) in 1939.

PART I

CHAPTER 1

1   Walter D. Morris (Mann [1918] 1983a) translates the last word of the title as 'nonpolitical'. Here and subsequently I prefer the customary rendering *unpolitical*, which is not only more nearly literal but also, I believe, more appropriate: whereas 'nonpolitical' denotes a stance of neutrality in relation to rival political interests, as in the familiar case of charitable organizations, 'unpolitical' describes a posture of moral detachment (usually critical) from politics as a form of social relationship.
2   Monday 16 September, 1918: 'What do they [the Allies] want? To drive out of us the experience of Goethe, Luther, Frederick the Great and Bismarck, so that we can "adjust ourselves to democracy"' (Mann 1983b: 5).
3   Sunday 5 October, 1918:

> My own view is that the worldwide triumph of democratic civilization in the political sphere is an accomplished fact, and that consequently, if the German spirit is to be preserved, one must recommend the separation of cultural and national life from politics, the complete detachment of one from the other. The thrust of my [*Reflections*] is against the fusion of the two realms, against the 'politicization' of Germany through the absolute domination, in the cultural sphere as well, of the victorious principle of democratic civilization.

(Mann, 1983b: 12)

4   The English translation renders *clerc* as '*clerk*' – an unhappy decision that not only does nothing to reduce the idiomatic disturbance but also fosters a spurious modern association with office and shop workers, and actually banalizes the sense of Benda's argument by introducing an ironic terminological hesitation with no counterpart in his French. Here, in singular usage, I simply copy Benda's own term, which presents no greater difficulty than any English substitute; the English collective noun *clerisy* perfectly renders his plural, *clercs*.

5   For some discussion of Mannheim's affinities with romantic medievalism, see Michael Löwy (1979: 87), and also Mannheim (1953: 123).

6   Leavis's *Mass Civilization and Minority Culture* was published by the Cambridge-based Minority Press. The version cited here appeared in the volume of essays *For Continuity* (Leavis 1933a). (The English translation of *La Rebelion de las Masas* appeared in 1932.)

CHAPTER 2

1   Woolf's essay, 'Middlebrow', which was composed in the form of a letter 'To the editor of the *New Statesman*', remained unpublished in her lifetime; the posthumous collection of essays in which it appeared, *The Death of the Moth* (Woolf 1942) gives no date, merely the editorial information that the letter was not sent. However, Woolf alludes unmistakably, in the continuous present, to Arnold Bennett's reviews of her books in the London *Evening Standard* in 1928–9; and the *New Statesman* took over the *Nation* and its title in early 1931. A date around 1930 seems plausible. (Her mocking comment on the British Broadcasting Corporation's 'control of the air' bears comparison with her friend E.M. Forster's public criticism of radio censorship in 1931: 'The Freedom of the BBC', *New Statesman and Nation* I (6) (New Series), 4 April 1931: pp. 209–10.

2   Compare in this regard her novel *Orlando* (1928).

3   Hélène Cixous insists on an identical discrimination within the notion of bisexuality in writing:

> In saying 'bisexual, hence neuter', I am referring to the classic conception of bisexuality, which, squashed under the emblem of castration fear and along with the fantasy of a 'total' being (though composed of two halves), would do away with the difference experienced as an operation incurring loss. ... To this self-effacing, merger-

type bisexuality, ... I oppose the *other bisexuality* ... that is, each one's location in self (*répérage de soi*) of the presence – variously manifest and insistent according to each person, male or female – of both sexes, non-exclusion either of the difference or of one.

(Cixous 1981: 254)

4   In *The Meaning of Culture*, an ephemeral book published in the same year (New York: Norton, 1929), the novelist John Cowper Powys exalted male–female complementarity as the most fertile ground of culture. He also insisted that every young woman in search of culture must have 'a room entirely her own' (pp. 134, 249, 272).

5   See in this connection Raymond Williams, 'The Bloomsbury Fraction' (1980: 148–69).

6   The phrase 'une promesse de bonheur' is Stendhal's (Marcuse [1937] 1972: 115).

CHAPTER 3

1   Bloomsbury was, for Eliot, a twentieth-century model of a traditional elite – and perhaps the last of its kind. See his obituary of Virginia Woolf in *Horizon*, May 1941, pp. 313–16.

CHAPTER 4

1   *Universities and Left Review* appeared in seven issues between Spring 1957 and Autumn 1959. The editors were Stuart Hall, Raphael Samuel, Gabriel Pearson and Charles Taylor.

2   *ULR* vol. I, no. 2, Summer 1957, p. 29.

3   Beginning from work in adult education classes in 1949, *Culture and Society* was written between 1952 and 1956.

4   Graham Martin's *Universities and Left Review* article, 'A Culture in Common' (1958: 70–9), was the moment, if there was one, when *Culture and Society* was canonized as a founding text for a New Left. The symbolic counterpoint was Terry Eagleton, *Criticism and Ideology*, London: NLB, 1976, Chapter 1.

5   'Comment', *Politics and Letters* vol. I, no. 1, Summer 1947, pp. 32–9.

6   'Editorial Note', *Arena* I (4).

7   *Politics and Letters: Interviews* (p. 98). Graham Pechey (1985) has emphasized the radically disruptive strategy of the book.

8 Indeed, 'there are no masses to save, to capture, or to direct' (Williams 1989: 18).

PART II

CHAPTER 1

1 This caveat should not be misconstrued as a case of 'empiricism'. '[My] experience of this English addiction to the concrete is that for the most part they are stuck in it', Williams wrote in 1961. 'Experience includes thought, and thought includes abstraction, and abstraction is in fact one of the glories of the human mind' (Williams 1989: 20) However, see also, in this connection, Catherine Gallagher's illuminating discussion of Williams's reading of money as a cultural form: 'Raymond Williams and Cultural Studies' (Gallagher 1995: 307–19).
2 *The Long Revolution* ([1961] 1965: 63) differs only in substituting 'study' for 'theory'; see further, 'Literature and Sociology' ([1971] 1980: 20), where that variant formulation recurs.

CHAPTER 2

1 He later used it again, as the title of his 1971 Reith Lectures for the BBC: *Only Connect: On Culture and Communication* (Hoggart 1972).
2 London: Hutchinson, 1964; and 'Liberal Studies', P. Whannel and P. Harcourt (eds) *Studies in the Teaching of Film Within Formal Education* (London: British Film Institute, 1964), pp. 10–27. See the interview 'The Formation of a Diasporic Intellectual' (1996f: 498).
3 The landmark texts were the collective volume *Resistance Through Rituals: Youth Subcultures in Postwar Britain* (Hall and Jefferson 1976) and Dick Hebdige's *Subcultures: The Meaning of Style* (1979).
4 The motif of a Marxism capable of discovering something new comes from another Marxist philosopher, Jean-Paul Sartre: 'Marxism possesses theoretical bases, it embraces all human activity; but it no longer *knows* anything' (Sartre 1963: 28).

CHAPTER 3

1 I have modified the verbs for syntactic context.
2 A recent bibliography of Hall's writings lists a further four versions of

this text (Hall 1973), plus one translation and a retrospective discussion of it (Hall 1996: 505–14). Reference here is mainly to what is probably the most widely circulated version (Hall 1980c: 128–38). Described as an 'edited extract', this version, the third, differs from the original in modifying and clarifying the discussion of semiotic concepts, especially 'denotation' and 'connotation', omitting punctual reference to Gramsci (though not his concepts), incorporating elements of a later discussion of Marx, and introducing a reference to Vološinov (1973) *Marxism and the Philosophy of Language*. It also omits a discussion of B-movie Westerns, in which Hall argues that gunfight scenarios are not 'about' violence (a staple official anxiety, then as now) but rather define and implement principles of masculine decorum (1973: 5–10). None of these textual differences is at stake in the present discussion.

3 *Mythologies* (Barthes 1972) appeared in 1957, *Marxism and the Philosophy of Language* (Vološinov 1973) in 1929.

4 John Kraniauskas (1998: 17) identifies the same conceptual slippage in the Open University's multi-volume course-book *Culture, Media and Identities* (1997), in which Hall had a leading role: 'the idea of "production" that forms part of the circuit of culture is more like work. ... It is ... production without relations of production'.

5 Indeed, futurist motifs were not foreign to Kulturkritik, as the case of Ortega illustrates. '... the human being has inevitably a futuristic constitution; that is to say, he lives primarily in the future and for the future' (Ortega 1932: 131n).

CHAPTER 4

1 *Cultural Studies* 6, 1, January 1992.

2 Compare Homi Bhabha: 'Culture only emerges as a problem, or a problematic, at the point where there is a loss of meaning in the contestation and articulation of everyday life, between classes, genders, races, nations' (Bhabba 1994: 340).

3 Stuart Hall and Martin Jacques, 'People Aid – A New Politics Sweeping the Land', *Marxism Today*, July 1985: pp. 10–14, cited in McGuigan 1992: 38.

4 Tony Bennett (1992: 34) has dismissed Hall's perception as 'wistful': 'to attribute such a function to an intellectual project which has [been] and continues to be based primarily in the academy suggests a misrecognition of its relations to its real conditions of existence that can

only be described as ideological.' For other criticisms, in different political and theoretical perspectives, see John Frow (1995) and Alan Sinfield (1997: 19–21).

PART III

1 The sub-title of this section borrows a phrase from Fredric Jameson (1993), a review essay on Grossberg *et al.* (1992).
2 Compare her historical fantasy *Orlando* (1928), in which the androgynous protagonist cannot forget the man s/he nearly met, who may have been Shakespeare.
3 As Lukács wrote years later, these were the years in which he and Mann parted spiritual company, Mann continuing in the romantic–pessimist tradition that had formed them both (Lukács 1964: 10).
4 Indeed, that problem was Lukács's own. Just a year earlier he had published an essay on 'The Old Culture and the New Culture', which attempted to synthesize a romantic critique of 'civilization' with his new-found belief in the redemptive potential of social revolution.
5 See *The Long Revolution* (Williams [1961] 1965), Part One, and, quite generally, *Marxism and Literature* (Williams 1997), where ideas akin to those of Lukács's *History and Class Consciousness* (1971) are central.
6 *Culture and Society* (Williams [1958] 1961: 17).
7 For lucid, scholarly accounts of Freud's 'splitting of the ego' and Melanie Klein's 'splitting of the object', see Laplanche and Pontalis (1988: 427–30).
8 For two dissenting judgements, see Ang (1992: 11–21) and O'Regan (1992: 395–408). Compare McGuigan (1996: 5), who distinguishes between 'cultural politics', to which he would refer Hall's arguments over black representation, and 'the politics of culture', which includes 'policy analysis and policy formulation'.

GLOSSARY

Authority designates any form of leadership asserted and accepted on non-coercive grounds – in contrast with 'power', which is inherently coercive.

Base and superstructure has long been a standard shorthand reference for the core thesis of Marx's materialist conception of history, or historical materialism. His claim was that economic relations play the fundamental part in the making and remaking of social relations as a whole. They are 'the real foundation' (he did not say 'base') on which the 'superstructures' of politics and culture arise.

Corporatism (from the Latin *corpus*, 'body') has designated social theories that model society (or the good society) on the body, seeing it as a complex of interdependent parts and functions, all making their necessary, mutually non-exchangeable contributions to the health of the whole. It is accordingly anti-individualist in temper (the notion of competition between parts of the body is absurd) and also anti-socialist (the notion of a struggle between the hands and the head is equally absurd – as are democracy and equality). In corporatist social schemes, the main constituents of the social body were often named 'corporations'. Hence the notion of a corporate or corporatist ethics of intellectual life, in which intellectuals as such are called to a common vocation as spiritual guides of society as a whole. The logic of corporatism is always, finally, authoritarian. The familar corporations of the present (say, publishing houses and universities), with their corporate missions and visions and values, seem a world away from the corporatist schemes of the 1930s, but they are not.

Discourse is, most simply and generally, language in action. In its strong, contemporary sense, of which my own usage is a variety, it asserts the priority of socially formed practices of language over the individuals who necessarily operate in and through them. A discourse is a more or less systematic set of forms, topics and procedures that regulates both the object of utterance – what is 'seen' and spoken of – and its subjects – the identities that 'we' assume, consciously or not, in practising it.

Metaculture, or 'metacultural discourse', is the term in which I summarize a critique of the intellectual traditions of 'culture' discussed here. Metacultural discourse is that in which 'culture' addresses its own generality – that is, the whole domain of meaning – and historical conditions of existence. Its fixed impulse is to displace politics as a form of social authority in the name of true and truly general authority, or 'culture'.

Organic has been an inescapable metaphor in European culture since the Romantics, usually connoting 'life', 'the natural', 'spontaneous growth', 'wholeness' and 'authenticity', in opposition to such (negative) values as 'system', 'calculation', 'schematism', 'rational construction' – all that is connoted by the equally tenacious metaphor of the 'mechanical'. This is its sense in the writing of F.R. Leavis and Richard Hoggart, for example. However, the senses of the metaphor that predominate in Part II of this volume are quite distinct. 'Organic' in Antonio Gramsci's usage means something like 'structurally or constitutionally necessary'. Thus the 'organic intellectuals' of a social class are those without which it could not sustain its distinctive form of life and practice. They are of and for the class they represent, in contrast with 'traditional intellectuals' who appear to constitute an independent social corporation (see above) in themselves. Likewise, the 'organic' aspects of a historical situation are those which are permanent features of a given form of society, in contrast with the 'conjunctural' aspects, which may be temporary, or merely 'accidental'.

Popular is a neutral or positive alternative to 'mass', which normally carries the connotations of homogeneity, mediocrity and passivity in matters of cultural preference. The relevant contraries are 'high' or 'elite' or, with a sharper political edge, 'dominant'.

Populism in the sense chiefly relevant here is the uncritical endorsement and adoption of the spontaneous tendencies (actual or imagined) of popular culture.

Subject in the only sense relevant here denotes the position of perceiving, speaking/listening and acting that I occupy at any time, the 'I' that I am or become, in a given context of discourse (see above). Discourse creates its subjects in that it establishes positions for actual individuals in the social order of meaning.

Symbol occurs in philosophy, linguistics, aesthetics, poetics and psychoanalysis in many senses, some of them perfect opposites. Here **symbolic** is used in a minimal, generic sense, as one word among others designating anything that makes or bears meaning.

Voluntarism designates any theory or pattern of activity that, implicitly or in effect, assumes the capacity of willed action to prevail against objective conditions.

BIBLIOGRAPHY

Adorno, T.W. ([1955] 1981) *Prisms: Cultural Criticism and Society*, Cambridge, Mass.: The MIT Press, 1981.

Althusser, L. (1969) *For Marx*, trans. Ben Brewster, London: Allen Lane.

Anderson, P. (1976) *Considerations on Western Marxism*, London: NLB.

—— (1980) *Arguments Within English Marxism*, London: Verso.

Ang, I. (1992) 'Dismantling "Cultural Studies"?' *Cultural Studies* 6, January: pp. 311–21.

—— (1996) 'Culture and Communication: Towards an Ethnographic Critique of Media Consumption in the Transnational Media System', in J. Storey (ed.) *What is Cultural Studies? A Reader*, London: Edward Arnold.

Arnold, M. ([1864] 1964) *Essays in Criticism*, London: Dent, 1964.

—— ([1869] 1932) *Culture and Anarchy*, J. Dover Wilson (ed.), Cambridge: Cambridge University Press, 1932.

Bakhtin, M.M. (1981) *The Dialogic Imagination: Four Essays*, M. Holquist (ed.), Austin: University of Texas Press.

Bantock, G.H. (1949) 'Mr Eliot and Education', *Scrutiny* XVI (1), March: pp. 64–70.

Barker, M. and Beezer, A. (eds) (1991) *Reading Into Cultural Studies*, London: Routledge.

Barnett, A. (1976) 'Raymond Williams and Marxism: A Rejoinder to Terry Eagleton', *New Left Review* 99, September–October: pp. 47–64.

Barthes, R. ([1957] 1972) *Mythologies*, trans. Annette Lavers, London: Jonathan Cape, 1972.

Bee, J. (1989) 'First Citizen of the Semiotic Democracy', *Cultural Studies* 3: pp. 353–9.

Bell, C. (1928) *Civilization: An Essay*, London: Chatto and Windus.

Benda, J. ([1928] 1969) *The Treason of the Intellectuals*, trans. R. Aldington, New York: W.W. Norton, 1969.

—— (1975) 'Préface de Julien Benda à l'édition de 1946', *La Trahison des clercs*, Paris: Grasset.

Benjamin, W. ([1936] 1970) 'The Work of Art in the Age of Mechanical Reproduction', in W. Benjamin *Illuminations*, London: Fontana, pp. 219–53.

—— ([1940] 1970) 'Theses on the Philosophy of History', in W. Benjamin *Illuminations*, London: Fontana, pp. 255–66.

—— (1970) *Illuminations*, London: Fontana.

Bennett, A. (1992) 'Putting Policy Into Cultural Studies', in L. Grossberg,

C. Nelson and P. Treichler (eds) *Cultural Studies*, New York and London: Routledge.

—— (1993) 'Useful Culture', in V. Blundell, J. Shepherd and I. Taylor (eds) *Relocating Cultural Studies*, London and New York: Routledge.

Bhabha, H.K. (1994) *The Location of Culture*, London: Routledge.

Birch, D. (1987) 'Publishing Populism', *Cultural Studies* 1 (1), January: pp. 127–35.

Blundell, V., Shepherd, J. and Taylor, I. (eds) (1993) *Relocating Cultural Studies*, London and New York: Routledge.

Bourdieu, P. (1993) *The Field of Cultural Production*, ed. and Introduction, R. Johnson, Oxford: Polity.

Bradbury, M. (1956) 'The Rise of the Provincials', *Antioch Review* XVI (4): pp. 469–77.

Brunsden, C. (1996) 'A Thief in the Night: Stories of Feminism in the 1970s at CCCS', in D. Morley and K.-H. Chen (eds) *Stuart Hall: Critical Dialogues in Cultural Studies*, London: Routledge, pp. 276–86.

Carey, J.W. (1997) 'Reflections on the Project of (American) Cultural Studies', in M. Ferguson and P. Golding *Cultural Studies in Question*, London: Sage, pp. 1–25.

Caudwell, C. (1937) *Illusion and Reality*, London: Macmillan.

—— ([1938 and 1949] 1971) *Studies and Further Studies in a Dying Culture*, New York: Monthly Review Press, 1971.

Centre for Contemporary Cultural Studies (1978) *On Ideology*, London: Hutchinson.

—— (1982) *The Empire Strikes Back*, London: Hutchinson.

Chambers, I. (1986) *Popular Culture: The Metropolitan Experience*, London: Methuen.

Cixous, H. (1981) 'The Laugh of the Medusa', in E. Marks and I. de Courtivron (eds) *New French Feminisms*, Brighton: Harvester.

Cormican, L.A. (1950) 'Mr Eliot and Social Biology', *Scrutiny* XVII (1), Spring: pp. 2–13.

Craik, J. (1987) 'The Road to Cultural Studies', *Cultural Studies* 1 (1), January: pp. 121–6.

de Certeau, M. (1980) *La culture au pluriel*, Paris: Christian Bourgois Editeur.

Eagleton, T. (1976) *Criticism and Ideology*, London: NLB.

Eliot, T.S. (1943) 'Notes Towards a Definition of Culture', *New English Weekly* XXII (14–17), 21 January–11 February: pp. 117–18, 128–30, 136–7, 145–6, respectively.

—— ([1948] 1962) *Notes Towards the Definition of Culture*, London: Faber and Faber, 1962.

Febvre, L. (1973) *A New Kind of History*, P. Burke (ed.), London: Routledge and Kegan Paul.

Ferguson, M. and Golding, P. (eds) (1997) *Cultural Studies in Question*, London: Sage.

Fiske, J. (1987) *Television Culture*, London: Methuen.

—— (1996) 'British Cultural Studies and Television', in J. Storey (ed.) *What is Cultural Studies? A Reader*, London: Edward Arnold, pp. 115–46.

Freud, S. ([1927] 1985) *The Future of an Illusion*, in *Civilization, Society and Religion*, The Pelican Freud Library, Volume 12, London: Penguin, 1985.

—— ([1930] 1985) *Civilization and Its Discontents*, in *Civilization, Society and Religion*, The Pelican Freud Library, Volume 12, London: Penguin, 1985.

—— (1985) *Civilization, Society and Religion*, The Pelican Freud Library, Volume 12, London: Penguin.

Freud, S. and Einstein, A. ([1932] 1985) *Why War?*, in *Civilization, Society and Religion*, The Pelican Freud Library, Volume 12, London: Penguin, 1985.

Frow, J. (1995) *Cultural Studies and Cultural Value*, Oxford: Clarendon.

Frow, J. and Morris, M. (1993) 'Australian Cultural Studies', in V. Blundell, J. Shepherd and I. Taylor (eds) *Relocating Cultural Studies*, London and New York: Routledge, pp. 344–67.

Gallagher, C. (1995) 'Raymond Williams and Cultural Studies', in C. Prendergast (ed.) *Cultural Materialism: On Raymond Williams*, Minneapolis: University of Minnesota Press, pp. 307–19.

Garnham, N. (1997) 'Political Economy and the Practice of Cultural Studies', in M. Ferguson and P. Golding (eds) *Cultural Studies in Question*, London: Sage, pp. 56–73.

Gilroy, P. (1988) *'There Ain't No Black in the Union Jack': The Cultural Politics of Race and Nation*, London: Hutchinson.

—— (1992) 'Cultural Studies and Ethnic Absolutism', in L. Grossberg, C. Nelson and P. Treichler (eds) *Cultural Studies*, New York and London: Routledge, pp. 187–98.

Gitlin, T. (1997) 'The Anti-political Populism of Cultural Studies', in M. Ferguson and P. Golding (eds) *Cultural Studies in Question*, London: Sage.

Gramsci, A. (1971) *Selections From the Prison Notebooks*, ed. and trans., Q. Hoare and G. Nowell-Smith, London: Lawrence and Wishart.

—— (1985) *Selections From Cultural Writings* ed. David Forgács and G. Nowell-Smith, London: Lawrence and Wishart.

Grossberg, L., Nelson, C. and Treichler, P. (eds) (1992) *Cultural Studies*, New York and London: Routledge.

Hall, S. (1958) 'A Sense of Classlessness', *Universities and Left Review* 1 (5), Autumn: pp. 26–32.

—— (1973) *Encoding and Decoding in the Television Discourse*, Birmingham: CCCS stencilled Occasional Paper.

—— (1980a) 'Cultural Studies and the Centre: Some Problematics and Problems', in S. Hall, D. Hobson, A. Lowe and P. Willis (eds) *Culture, Media Language: Working Papers in Cultural Studies 1972–79*, London: Routledge, 1992, pp. 15–47.

—— (1980b) 'Cultural Studies: Two Paradigms', *Media, Culture and Society*, no. 2, 1980: pp. 57–72.

—— (1980c) 'Encoding and Decoding', in S. Hall, D. Hobson, A. Lowe and P. Willis, *Culture, Media Language: Working Papers in Cultural Studies 1972–79*, London: Routledge, [1980] 1992, pp. 128–38.

—— (1989) 'The Meaning of New Times', in S. Hall and M. Jacques (eds) (1989) *New Times: The Changing Face of Politics in the 1990s*, London: Lawrence and Wishart.

—— (1990) 'The Emergence of Cultural Studies and the Crisis of the Humanities', *October* 53: pp. 11–23.

—— (1996a) 'The Problem of Ideology: Marxism Without Guarantees' [1983], in D. Morley and K.-H. Chen (eds) *Stuart Hall: Critical Dialogues in Cultural Studies*, London: Routledge, pp. 25–46.

—— (1996b) 'On Postmodernism and Articulation' [1986] in D. Morley and K.-H. Chen (eds) *Stuart Hall: Critical Dialogues in Cultural Studies*, London: Routledge, pp. 131–50.

—— (1996c) 'Gramsci's Relevance for the Study of Race and Ethnicity' [1986], in D. Morley and K.-H. Chen (eds) *Stuart Hall: Critical Dialogues in Cultural Studies*, London: Routledge, pp. 411–40.

—— (1996d) 'New Ethnicities' [1989], in D. Morley and K.-H. Chen (eds) *Stuart Hall: Critical Dialogues in Cultural Studies*, London: Routledge, pp. 441–9.

—— (1996e) 'Cultural Studies and Its Theoretical Legacies' [1992], in D. Morley and K.-H. Chen (eds) *Stuart Hall: Critical Dialogues in Cultural Studies*, London: Routledge, pp. 262–75.

—— (1996f) 'The Formation of a Diasporic Intellectual' [1992] in D. Morley and K.-H. Chen (eds) *Stuart Hall: Critical Dialogues in Cultural Studies*, London: Routledge, pp. 484–503.

—— (1996g) 'What Is This "Black" in Black Popular Culture?' [1992], in D. Morley and K.-H. Chen (eds) *Stuart Hall: Critical Dialogues in Cultural Studies*, London: Routledge, pp. 465–75.

—— (1996h) 'For Allon White: Metaphors of Transformation' [1993], in D. Morley and K.-H. Chen (eds) *Stuart Hall: Critical Dialogues in Cultural Studies*, London: Routledge, pp. 287–305.

—— (1997) 'Culture and Power' (interview), *Radical Philosophy* 86, November–December: pp. 24–41.

Hall, S. and Jacques, M. (eds) (1983) *The Politics of Thatcherism*, London: Lawrence and Wishart.

—— (1989) *New Times: the Changing Face of Politics in the 1990s*, London: Lawrence and Wishart.

Hall, S. and Jefferson, A. (1976) *Resistance Through Rituals: Youth Subcultures in Postwar Britain*, London: Hutchinson.

Hall, S., Hobson, D. Lowe, A. and Willis, P. (1980) *Culture, Media Language: Working Papers in Cultural Studies 1972–79*, London: Hutchinson; London: Routledge (1992).

Hebdige, R. (1979) *Subcultures: The Meaning of Style*, London: Methuen.

—— (1988) 'Banalarama', *New Statesman and Society*, 9 December.

Heinemann, M. (1985) 'The People's Front and the Intellectuals', in J. Fyrth (ed.) *Britain, Fascism and the Popular Front*, London: Lawrence and Wishart, pp. 157–86.

Herder, J.G. von ([1774] 1969) *Herder on Social and Political Culture*, ed. and trans. F.M. Barnard, Cambridge: Cambridge University Press, 1969.

Hobsbawm, E. (1994) *Age of Extremes: The Short Twentieth Century 1914–1991*, London: Michael Joseph.

Hoggart, R. (1958) *The Uses of Literacy*, Harmondsworth: Penguin.

—— (1970a) *Speaking to Each Other, I: About Society*, London: Chatto and Windus.

—— (1970b) *Speaking to Each Other, II: About Literature*, London: Chatto and Windus.

—— (1972) *Only Connect: On Culture and Communication*, London: Chatto and Windus.

—— (1990) *A Sort of Clowning. Life and Times vol. II: 1940–1959*, London: Chatto and Windus.

—— (1992) *An Imagined Life. Life and Times vol. III: 1959–91*, London: Chatto and Windus.

Jameson, F. (1993) 'On "Cultural Studies"', *Social Text* 34: pp. 17–52.

Johnson, R. (1996) 'What Is Cultural Studies Anyway?' in J. Storey (ed.) *What Is Cultural Studies? A Reader*, London: Edward Arnold.

Jordan, G. and Weedon, C. (1995) *Cultural Politics*, Oxford: Blackwell, 1995.

Kojecký, R. (1971) *T.S. Eliot's Social Criticism*, London: Faber and Faber.

Kraniauskas, J. (1998) 'Globalization Is Ordinary: The Transnationalization of Cultural Studies', *Radical Philosophy* 90, July–August.

Kraus, K. (1984) *In These Great Times: A Karl Kraus Reader*, ed. H. Zohn, Manchester: Carcanet.

Laplanche, J. and Pontalis, J.-B. (1988) *The Language of Psychoanalysis*, trans. D. Nicholson-Smith, London: Karnac Books and the Institute of Psychoanalysis.

Leavis, F.R (1930) *Mass Civilization and Minority Culture*, Cambridge: Minority Press; reprinted in Leavis, F.R. (1933a).

—— (1933a) *For Continuity*, Cambridge: Minority Press.

—— (1933b) 'Restatement for Critics', *Scrutiny* I (4), March: 315–23.

Lefranc, G. (1965) *Histoire du Front populaire*, Paris: Payot.

Leroy, G. and Roche, A. (1986) *Les écrivains et le Front populaire*, Paris: Presse de la Fondation Nationale des Sciences Politiques.

Lewis, G. I. (1957) 'Candy-flossing the Celtic Fringe', *Universities and Left Review* 2 (1), Summer.

Lloyd, D. and Thomas, P. (1998) *Culture and the State*, New York and London: Routledge.

Lottmann, H.R. (1982) *The Left Bank: Writers, Artists and Politics From the Popular Front to the Cold War*, London: Heinemann.

Löwy, M. (1979) *Georg Lukács – From Romanticism to Bolshevism*, London: NLB.

Lukács, G. (1964) *Essays on Thomas Mann*, London: Merlin Press.

—— (1971) *History and Class Consciousness*, London: Merlin Press.

McGuigan, J. (1992) *Cultural Populism*, London and New York: Routledge.

—— (1996) *Culture and the Public Sphere*, London: Routledge.

McLeish, J. (1957) 'Variant Readings', *Universities and Left Review* 1 (2), Summer.

MacKillop, I. (1995) *F.R. Leavis: A Life in Criticism*, London: Penguin.

McRobbie, A. (1996) 'Looking Back at New Times and Its Critics', in D. Morley and K.-H. Chen (eds) *Stuart Hall: Critical Dialogues in Cultural Studies*, London: Routledge, pp. 238–61.

Mann, T. ([1918] 1983a) *Reflections of a Nonpolitical Man*, trans. W.D. Morris, New York: Frederick Unger, 1983.

—— (1983b) *Diaries 1918–1939*, trans. R. Winston and C. Winston, London: André Deutsch, 1983.

Mannheim, K. (1936) *Ideology and Utopia*, trans. L. Wirth and E. Shils, London: Routledge and Kegan Paul.

—— (1940) *Man and Society in an Age of Reconstruction*, London: Kegan Paul, Trench, Trubner.

—— (1953) 'Conservative Thought', *Essays in Sociology and Social Psychology*, London: Routledge and Kegan Paul.

Marcuse, H. ([1937] 1972) 'The Affirmative Character of Culture', *Negations*, Harmondsworth: Penguin, 1972, pp. 88–133.

Marks, E. and de Courtivron, I. (eds) (1981) *New French Feminisms*, Brighton: Harvester.

Martin, G. (1958) 'A Culture in Common', *Universities and Left Review* 1 (5), Autumn: pp. 70–9.

Marx, K. ([1859] 1970) 'Preface to *A Contribution to the Critique of Political Economy*' (1859) Karl Marx and Frederick Engels, *Selected Works*, London: Lawrence and Wishart, 1970, pp. 180–4.

—— (1973) *Grundrisse: Foundations of the Critique of Political Economy (Rough Draft)* trans. M. Nicolaus, Harmondsworth: Penguin, 1973.

—— ([1869] 1976) *Capital, Volume 1*, London: Penguin, 1976.

Mellor, A. (1992) 'Discipline and Punish? Cultural Studies in Britain at the Crossroads', *Media, Culture and Society* 14 (4), October: pp. 663–70.

Mencken, H.L. ([1919] 1936) *The American Language: An Inquiry into the Development of English in the United States*, New York: Knopf, 1919; 4th edn 1936; supplements 1945, 1948.

Modlewski, T. (ed.) (1986) *Studies in Entertainment: Critical Approaches to Mass Culture*, Bloomington, Indiana: Indiana University Press.

Moriarty, M. (1995) '"The Longest Cultural Journey": Raymond Williams and French Theory', in C. Prendergast (ed.) *Cultural Materialism: On Raymond Williams*, Minneapolis: University of Minnesota Press, pp. 91–116.

Morley, D. (1997) 'Theoretical Orthodoxies: Textualism, Constructivism and the "Ethnography" in Cultural Studies', in M. Ferguson and P. Golding (eds) *Cultural Studies in Question*, London: Sage, pp. 121–38.

Morpurgo, W.E. (1979) *Allen Lane, King Penguin: A Biography*, London: Allen Lane.

Morris, M. ([1988] 1996) 'Banality in Cultural Studies', in J. Storey (ed.)

    What Is Cultural Studies? A Reader, London: Edward Arnold, 1996, pp. 147–67.

Mulhern, F. (1979) *The Moment of 'Scrutiny'*, London: NLB.

—— ([1990] 1998) 'English Reading', in *The Present Lasts a Long Time: Essays in Cultural Politics*, Cork: Cork University Press and Notre Dame: University of Notre Dame Press, 1998.

New Left Review (1977) *Western Marxism – A Critical Reader*, London: NLB.

O'Regan, T. (1992) '(Mis)Taking Policy: Notes on the Cultural Policy Debate', *Cultural Studies* 6 (3), October: pp. 395–408.

Ortega y Gasset, J. (1932) *The Revolt of the Masses*, London: Allen and Unwin.

Orwell, G. (1961) *Collected Essays, Journalism and Letters*, vol. 1, London: Secker and Warburg.

—— (1970a) *Collected Essays, Journalism and Letters*, vol. 2, Harmonds-worth: Penguin.

—— (1970b) *Collected Essays, Journalism and Letters*, vol. 3, Harmonds-worth: Penguin.

—— (1970c) *Collected Essays, Journalism and Letters*, vol. 4, Harmonds-worth: Penguin.

—— ([1936] 1970d) *The Road to Wigan Pier*, London: Penguin, 1970.

O'Shea, A. and Schwartz, B. (1987) 'Reconsidering Popular Culture', *Screen* 28 (3), Summer.

Pechey, G. (1985) '*Scrutiny*, English Marxism, and the Work of Raymond Williams', *Literature and History* 11 (1), Spring: pp. 65–76.

Pocock, D.F. (1950) 'Symposium on Mr Eliot's Notes (III)', *Scrutiny* XVII (3), Autumn: pp. 273–6.

Powys, J.C. (1929) *The Meaning of Culture*, New York: Norton.

Prendergast, C. (ed.) (1995) *Cultural Materialism: On Raymond Williams*, Minneapolis: University of Minnesota Press.

Preston, P. (1987) 'The Creation of the Popular Front in Spain', in H. Graham and P. Preston (eds) *The Popular Front in Europe*, London: Macmillan Press.

Rustin, M. (1989) 'The Trouble With New Times', in S. Hall and M. Jacques (eds) *New Times: The Changing Face of Politics in the 1990s*, London: Lawrence and Wishart.

Samuel, R. (1994) *Theatres of Memory Vol. 1: Past and Present in Contemporary Culture*, London: Verso.

Sartre, J.-P. (1963) *The Problem of Method*, trans. H.E. Barnes, London: Methuen.

Schwartz, B. (1989) 'Popular Culture: The Long March', *Cultural Studies* 3 (2), May: pp. 250–5.

Shiach, M. (1989) *Discourse on Popular Culture: Class, Gender and History in Cultural Analysis 1730 to the Present Day*, Cambridge: Polity.

Sinfield, A. (1997) *Culture and Authority*, São Paulo, Working Papers in British Studies, 3.

Spender, S. (1953) 'Comment: On Literary Movements', *Encounter* 1 (2): pp. 66–8.

Steele, T. (1997) *The Emergence of Cultural Studies 1945–65: Cultural Politics, Adult Education and the English Question*, London: Lawrence and Wishart.

Storey, J. (1996) *What Is Cultural Studies? A Reader*, London: Edward Arnold.

Stratton, J. and Ang, I. (1996) 'On the Impossibility of a Global Cultural Studies: "British" Cultural Studies in an "International Frame"', in D. Morley and K.-H. Chen (eds) *Stuart Hall: Critical Dialogues in Cultural Studies*, London: Routledge, pp. 361–91.

Thompson, E.P. (1961) 'The Long Revolution' and 'The Long Revolution – II', *New Left Review* 9 and 10, May–June and July–August: pp. 24–33 and 34–9, respectively.

Trilling, L. (1939) *Matthew Arnold*, New York: Norton.

Valéry, P. (1948) *Monsieur Teste*, trans. J. Mathews, New York: Knopf.

—— (1963) *History and Politics*, ed. J. Mathews, London: Routledge and Kegan Paul.

Vološinov, V.N. ([1929] 1973) *Marxism and the Philosophy of Language*, New York: Seminar Press, 1973.

White, L.A. (1975) *The Concept of Cultural Systems*, New York and London: Columbia University Press.

Williams, R. (1957) 'Working Class Culture', *Universities and Left Review* 2 (1), Summer: pp. 31–2.

—— ([1958] 1961) *Culture and Society 1780–1950*, Harmondsworth: Penguin, 1961.

—— ([1961] 1965) *The Long Revolution*, Harmondsworth: Penguin, 1965.

—— (1977) *Marxism and Literature*, Oxford: Oxford University Press.

—— (1979) *Politics and Letters: Interviews With New Left Review*, London: NLB.

—— (1980) *Problems in Materialism and Culture*, London: Verso.

—— (1981) *Culture*, London: Fontana.

—— (1983) *Towards 2000*, London: Chatto and Windus.

—— (1989) *Resources of Hope: Culture, Democracy, Socialism*, edited by R. Gable, London: Verso.

Williams, R. and Hoggart, R. (1960) 'Working-class Attitudes' (a conversation), *New Left Review* 1, January–February: pp. 26–30.

Williamson, J. (1986) 'The Problems of Being Popular', *New Socialist* 41, September: pp. 14–15.

Woolf, V. ([1929] 1977) *A Room of One's Own*, London: Grafton.

—— (1942) *The Death of the Moth*, London, Hogarth Press.

—— (1967) *Collected Essays*, vol. 4, London: Hogarth Press.

Women's Studies Group, CCCS (1978) *Women Take Issue: Aspects of Women's Subordination*, London: Hutchinson.

Wright, P. (1985) *On Living in an Old Country: The National Past in Contemporary Britain*, London: Verso.

INDEX